THE STORY OF SKIING

Glass engraving by Gernot Schluifer, Kitzbühel, Austria.

THE STORY OF SKIING

SKIING

PAINTINGS BY Robert Guy

WRITTEN BY Ranulf Rayner

DAVID & CHARLES
Newton Abbot   London

To the memory of Nigel Hollis, late marketing director of my
publishers David & Charles, whose unselfish enthusiasm
encouraged me to embark on this library of sporting books,
and to Sir Arnold Lunn whose inspiration placed Alpine skiing
on the map.

A donation from the proceeds of this book will be given to the
Brotherhood of St Christopher

LEVAVI OCULOS

Let me give thanks, dear Lord,
in the frailty of age
for the beloved mountains of my youth,
for the challenge of rock
and for the joy of skiing,
for the friends with whom I climbed and skied,
and above all, dear Lord,
for those moments of revelation
when the temporal beauty of the mountains
reinforces my faith in the Eternal Beauty
which is not subject to decay.

Arnold Lunn (1888–1974). An epitaph

British Library Cataloguing in Publication Data
Rayner, Ranulf, 1935–
The story of skiing.
1. Skiing
I. Title II. Guy, Robert
796.93

ISBN 0 7153 9365 0

Line illustrations by Ethan Danielson
Book designed by Michael Head
© Ranulf Rayner 1989

Typeset by ABM Typographics Ltd, Hull
and printed in Singapore
by Saik Wah Press
for David & Charles Publishers plc
Brunel House   Newton Abbot   Devon

CONTENTS

St Christoph.

FOREWORD

Of all the great outdoor sports, skiing is perhaps the most dramatic. Yet, surprisingly, only a few artists have ever made a positive attempt to bring the subject alive.

At the Rijksmuseum in Amsterdam we have many beautiful paintings of the seventeenth century of winter scenes including works by Adam van Breen of skaters and early ice-hockey players and by Adriaan van de Velde, whose family are perhaps better known for their glorious scenes of sailing craft. But paintings of skiers are completely unfamiliar to the Dutch.

As a citizen of probably the flattest country in the world, it may seem astonishing to some that Ranulf Rayner has invited me to write the foreword to his story of skiing, but he, like others I have met on the slopes, knows of my love for this great sport with which I still remain totally enthralled.

I started skiing seriously during our honeymoon in Poland and Austria, and I belong to those skiers who never took a real lesson from scratch. After the war I skied in Zermatt, Grindelwald, Wengen and later in St Anton. For the last twenty-eight years we have been skiing in Lech. From the village of St Anton it is possible, by taking the cable to the Galzig, to ski down to the historic hamlet of St Christoph which guards one of the most important gateways in the Alps, the notorious Arlberg Pass. Here in 1986 we celebrated the 600th anniversary of the Brotherhood of St Christopher.

The Arlberg Pass, for all its beauty, has more than a streak of wickedness. Many of the early travellers who faced its avalanches, rockfalls and savage storms, were saved from a frozen grave only by the magnanimity of a one-time swineherd, Heinrich of Kempten, who in 1386 built a refuge which, albeit reconstructed, survives today as the famous St Christoph Hospice. The Brotherhood of St Christopher, founded at about the same time, has carried on Heinrich's charitable work in the high mountains ever since. On 3 January 1901 a number of hardy Austrians met in the kitchens of the hospice to form the Ski-Club Arlberg, now hailed as the 'cradle of Alpine skiing'. I am very proud to have been awarded the Gold Medal of the club.

It has been my privilege to be friends with these wonderful people and their children and with them to have seen the glistening slopes of the Arlberg become the bountiful land of the 'Skipetars'. Ranulf Rayner has conveyed the difficulties and the exhilaration of this wonderful sport and Robert Guy's paintings have captured the beauty of being in the mountains on skis. All who read this book will truly enjoy it.

BERNHARD, PRINCE OF THE NETHERLANDS

7

The Spread of World Skiing

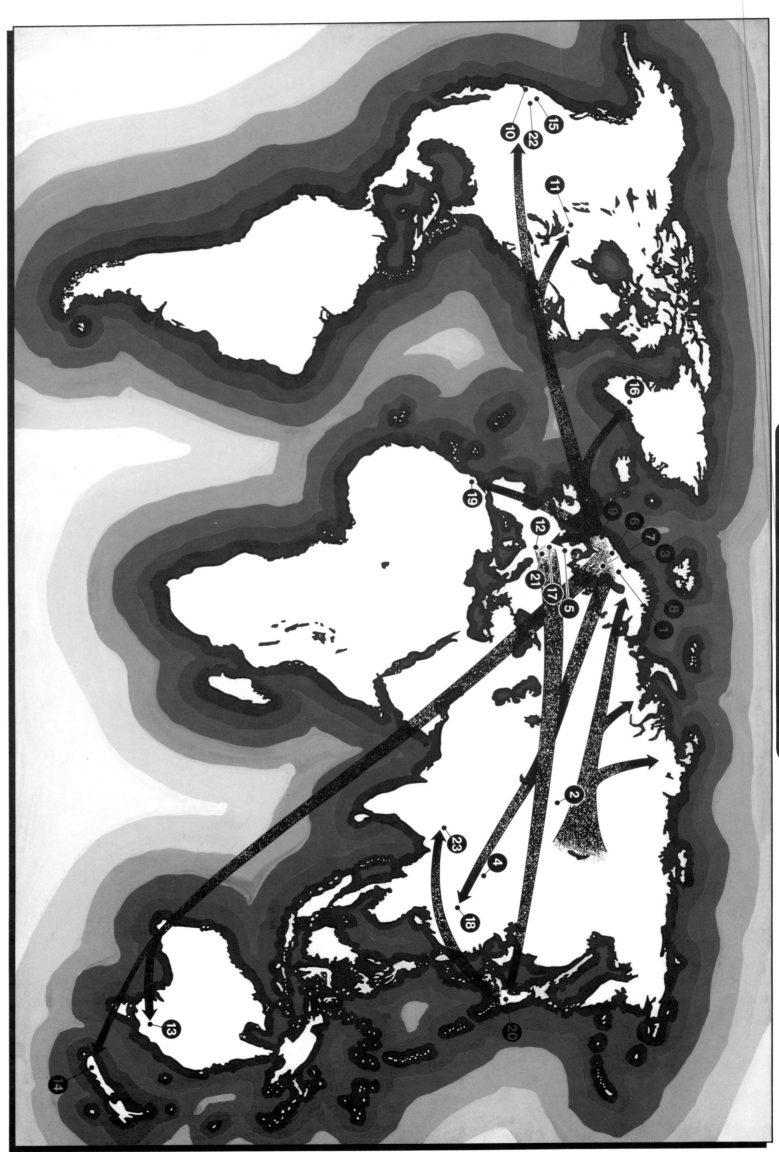

1 **2500 BC** Estimated date of 'Hoting Ski' discovered in a Swedish peat bog

2 **2500 BC** Skis found in the Altai mountains in Khasakstan, Russia

3 **2000 BC** Estimated date of rock impression of skier found at Roedoey, Norway

4 **800** Earliest written account of skis in history of T'ang Dynasty

5 **1070** Bishop Adam of Bremen sights northern hunters 'home on bent boards'

6 **1206** Two Norwegian 'Birkebeiner' ski King Sverre's infant son to safety

7 **1520** Gustav Vasa skis to Mora, Sweden, to lead his troops against the Danes

8 **1843** First organised ski race, cross-country from Tromsoe in Norway

9 **1825** The *Restoration* sails from Stavanger to the New World carrying skis

10 **1849** Norwegian sailors looking for gold set out with skis from San Francisco

11 **1857** A Norwegian labourer brings skiing to Ontario, Canada

12 **1859** Skis first seen in Switzerland at Sils Maria in the Engadine

13 **1861** First ski club in the world founded in Kiandra, Australia

14 **1862** Norwegian miners bring skis to the Otago goldfields in New Zealand

15 **1867** The first ski club in the United States formed at La Porte, California

16 **1888** Fridtjof Nansen crosses Greenland for the first time, on skis

17 **1891** Mathias Zdarsky starts skiing in the Black Forest region of Germany

18 **1899** Norwegian missionaries take their skis to China

19 **1904** Norwegian soldiers use skis training in the Atlas Mountains, Africa

20 **1911** Skiing introduced from Europe to Japan

21 **1934** The first T-bar ski lift installed, at Davos in Switzerland

22 **1936** The first chair lift built at Sun Valley, United States of America

23 **1970** Yuichiro Miura, Japan, skis down Mount Everest

INTRODUCTION

Some years ago, while recovering from a particularly horrifying skiing accident, I hobbled into an office in London on crutches. 'What d'yer want?' said a telephone-festooned Harry Salzman. 'How about shooting *On Her Majesty's Secret Service*', I brazenly replied, 'as the next James Bond film?' And so began my brief but glorious association with the film industry in no lesser role than advising on the skiing sequences, doubling Mr Blofeld with my friend the then British Ski Champion, Jeremy Palmer-Tomkinson, and planting a forest of felled pine trees for the cameras of the renowned skier Willy Bogner which, because of their extreme angle, made the shallow-built bob run appear impossibly steep.

Languishing in the Canton Hospital in Chur two days after my skiing accident I had asked my surgeon, the much respected Dr Algover, why I was receiving so much personal attention from the young nurses; 'they only seem to speak that curious language Romansh', I somewhat foolishly complained. 'Because', he replied, 'the hospital is so full of broken bones that we had to put you in the women's ward, so you are quite a novelty.' A lot of snow has melted since and I doubt that many subsequent male inmates have enjoyed the same treatment. No longer, I suspect, are the beds strewn with shattered bodies; the continued improvement in safety bindings has put paid to all that. Now, except where the volume of skiers on the piste is positively dangerous, many mountain clinics wait more anxiously for patients with corns and ingrowing toenails than for the rumble of the 'blood waggons'.

Recent changes in other aspects of the sport have been equally far-reaching. The exploits of Mr Blofeld and his henchmen now look tame compared with the current television pictures of downhill racing, and Mr Bond, then doubled on skis by the formidable downhiller Luki Leitner, would hardly stand out, except as an eccentric, in today's queue for the super-quad chairlift. Clothes have exploded into colour, boots are no longer made of decent leather but rather of plastic, and one ski, it seems for many young skiers, is better than two. Even the snow itself may be successfully made by machine. Just the rock is for real – or is it? The Japanese, who now have more skiers per head than any other nation, are already working on snow-covered indoor artificial mountains.

My story of skiing begins long before the age of plastic, almost in the Ice Age. It follows the early skiers and their wanderings and then traces the spread of the sport of skiing to most of the mountain ranges on earth. It considers *ski-laufen*, as the German word describes the Scandinavian conceived sport of cross-country skiing, and *ski-fahren* or downhill skiing as developed by the British, who have no mountains, and by other great sporting nations fortunate enough to have plenty of them. In those liftless days you had to have a strong dose of ski fever to climb for hours on end only to descend in a matter of minutes. But there are still those who enjoy the climbing as much as the descent and others who feel happier with a parachute – in either direction. The book investigates how the sport has been developed to suit a wide variety of different tastes and it unashamedly sets out to wet the appetites of all those who have thought of going skiing but never tried it, and the many who have skied but who have never enjoyed half of it.

Sir Arnold Lunn, who pioneered the sport in the Alps, once wrote about an evening climb on skis:

A full moon sailed into the sky just as we cut the last track to the hut in the wind-packed powder. Far away in the north, gleaming like burnished silver, the mountains merged into the soft radiance of the moonlit sky. In summer the music of the valley river and the murmur of glacier streams recalls the world of change, but no such sounds disturb the austere silence of night among the lonely places of the Alps in winter. In all that vast snowscape the track cut by our skis was the only link with the world of living things.

How many skiers stop to breathe in the pure mountain air and to delight in the majesty of the landscape? How many escape totally from the beaten track, not just into the virgin powder and to slopes briefly unscarred by man, but to where there are no lifts and no signposts, and where a sudden change in the weather may transform, as Lunn put it, "an easy expedition into a grim struggle for survival"?

No photographer can do justice to this varied and glorious sport and yet few painters of skiing scenes have succeeded either. The romantic revival of the early nineteenth century resulted in a proliferation of mountain art but, even by the 1920s, skiing paintings were the province almost entirely of the caricaturist and the fashion artist. Since then, principally in America, only a handful of brave painters have attempted to tackle a subject made more difficult by its unusual combination of sometimes awesome speed and absolute tranquillity. Now Robert Guy, a young painter with a great future, has set out, in his own dramatic way, to put the matter right.

EARLY YEARS

Over four thousand years ago some determined nomadic tribesman, whose hunting ground lay in the Ural Mountains or in the arctic plains of northern Europe, threw away his clumsy snow-shoes and stepped onto a pair of skis. History tells us little about the early skis or who invented them, and to find out would be no less difficult than trying to discover the makers of the first rude attempt at the wheel. But although the origins of the ski have been lost in the mists of time, it is safe to assume that the idea of gliding on snow was simply a progression from the weary business of donning snow-shoes and plodding after the ever elusive elk, wolf or wandering herds of reindeer.

Probably the oldest rock art ever discovered, in a

The rescue of young Haakon Haakonsson by two *Birkebeiner* or 'Birchlegs' (their leggings were fashioned of birch bark),
dramatised by a latter-day artist.

Norwegian cave, represents a skier, and in the Swedish marshes geologists have found fragments of skis, such as those at Hoting, which have been pollen dated to as far back as 2500 BC. Stone Age man seems to have had a wide choice of skis, the Arctic type (two short skis) being most popular in Russia, the Nordic type (two long thin skis) in Finnish Lapland, and the Osterdal type (one long ski for gliding and one short ski for pushing) in Norway and southern Sweden. At last, with the invention of the ski, reindeer ranching had become a reality and hunting over the frozen wastes such a worthwhile occupation that tribesmen, when they died, were no longer buried with any weapon other than their one trusty pointed ski-stick. In AD 555 the Byzantine historian Procopius mentioned the Laplanders as *skridfinnen* (gliding) Finns and in their national poem the *Kalevala*, the Finns' great hero

Wolf hunting in Lapland. The ski-pole comes in handy.

Lemminkainen had a ski-stick which caused smoke to rise every time he touched the snow with it.

Norwegian history is laced with many stories of skiing, and since 1932 a cross-country ski race, the *Birkebeinerlauf*, has been held every year to commemorate the episode in 1206 when, during the Baglern Revolt two valiant *Birkebeiner*, King Sverre's faithful bodyguards, skied with the infant prince Haakon Haakonsson, later to make his country famous, to safety across the snow-covered Dovre Mountains. In 1520, another epic journey took place in Sweden when Gustav Vasa (who became King Gustavus Eriksson) returned 55 miles (89km) on skis from Sälen to Mora in order to lead his people against the invading Danes, an exploit remembered today by a cross-country ski race which is still the longest in the world.

Thomas à Becket's secretary wrote in 1180 that men with bones tied to their feet 'doe slide as swiftly as a birde flyeth in the aire', and this did not go unnoticed by the military. In the year 1200, at the time of the Battle of Oslo, King Sverre of Sweden already had an élite reconnaissance company equipped with skis. In 1274 the hunting of deer on skis was forbidden in Norway and, as skiing for the pot became generally less of a necessity, the army took over as skiing's principal aficionados. In 1733 the first ski manual was produced, and in 1747 a Norwegian corps of ski-runners was formed with companies each of 100 men. When war was declared with Sweden in 1808, Norway mobilised over 2,000 regular ski troops.

In the year 1070, Bishop Adam of Bremen returned from a visit to Scandinavia with an extraordinary tale of seeing wild hunters 'borne on bent boards'. During the fifteenth and sixteenth centuries ski-running was frequently alluded to by those who, spurred on by the spirit of adventure, travelled to the farthest north and

A Norwegian soldier of about 1780. Note the long and the short ski or *andor*, which was often covered in animal fur to stop it sliding backwards.

returned to write about their experiences in books now made possible by the new printing presses. One, an Italian named Francesco Negri, makes it clear that in 1664 he was probably the first ever central-European to wear 'skie'. However, by the beginning of the nineteenth century, skis were still being used principally by the Scandinavian armies. Socially, skiing was quite unacceptable and as far as most were concerned it was a poor form of transport used otherwise by farmers and labourers.

It is interesting that at this stage skiing did not spread south into Central Europe, but west into North America instead. The first skiers in the New World probably sailed from Stavanger on the steamship *Restoration* which, with a passenger list composed entirely of miners and lumbermen, arrived off California in October 1825. In 1857 a Norwegian labourer was responsible for introducing skis to the Canadians and it was not long before they and their American neighbours were regarding skiing as more of a relaxation than a necessity. In 1867 the first American ski club was inaugurated at La Porte in California.

The finish of a military race held outside Stockholm, Sweden, in 1886.

Early ski resort at La Porte, California – note the starting gong.

School children at La Porte, California. Boys were given longer skis!

The first skier in America of any consequence was John A. Thompson, born Jon Thorenson at Telemark in Norway in 1827, and better remembered as 'Snowshoe Thompson.' For years he carried the mail over the high sierra from Genoa to Hangtown in California, a distance of some 90 miles (145km), on a monstrous pair of 12ft (4m) skis. His only means of control was a heavy ski-pole, an accepted method of braking that continued well into the twentieth century.

SKIS ARRIVE IN CENTRAL EUROPE

Surprisingly it was not until 1860, one year before the first ski club in the world was founded at Kiandra in Australia, and only two years before skiing reached New Zealand, that skis were first seen, but not used, in Central Europe, at Sils Maria in the Engadine, Switzerland. The accounts of those times are remarkably blurred, but it is known that in 1864 Johannes Badrutt, at the Kulm Hotel in St Moritz, only a few miles further up the valley, was probably the first hotelier to invite foreigners, a party of four English gentlemen, to enjoy a winter holiday in the Alps. That they remained with him until the snow melted, if not an indication of the winter sports'

The Old Jump.

Founder members of the Christiania Ski Club, 1877.

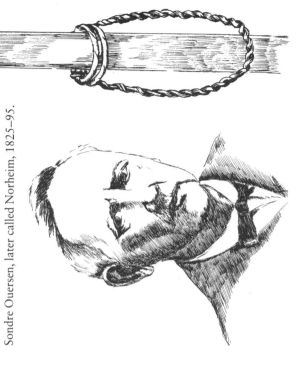

Sondre Ouersen, later called Norheim, 1825–95.

fever which was to follow, could hardly be attributed solely to his generosity or an addiction to his cellar.

Skiing emerged as a sport not in the Alps, however, but closer to where it had all started, and largely due to one man, Sondre Norheim. Born at Morgedal in the Telemark province of western Norway in 1825, Sondre was obsessed with skiing from an early age and, although virtually illiterate, by 1866 had perfected two methods of turning downhill and the most exciting modifications to ski design since the Stone Age. In 1840 Sondre had discovered that by landing on sloping ground he could risk jumping further than any man before him and thus he is credited with being the inventor of the modern ski jump. The skis he designed had three novel features: they were 'waisted' or made narrower under the binding to give better control; they were shorter being under 8ft (2.5m) in length, and instead of just a toe-piece the bindings had an additional heel-strap of twisted willow. In 1866 Sondre demonstrated his novel turns which he named the 'telemark' and the 'christiania', and two years later he leaped 60ft (18m) to win the jumping competition at Christiania, now

Oslo (later known as the notorious Holmenkollen jump). The Norwegian press was full of the story and within a few years skis of unequal length, which were still popular, had vanished from the scene.

The skis Sondre Norheim designed have remained almost unaltered, except in material, until today, the christiania is here to stay and the telemark turn is surprisingly staging a revival. But it required more than the *Christiania News* to spread the story of skiing into Central Europe and it was not until the great arctic explorer Fridtjof Nansen's book *Paa Ski Over Grönland* was published, particularly the German edition of 1891, that skiing fired the imagination of a few gallant gentlemen in the Alps.

Amongst those who were intrigued with Nansen's book was an Austrian adventurer, Mathias Zdarsky. Determined to try out the Norwegian's ideas, he spent several winters skiing alone in the Black Forest, it is said without meeting another skier. In 1896 he published his own book entitled *Lilienfelder Schilauf-Technik* in which he made the first methodical analysis of a turn he had invented, now known universally as the stem turn. A follower wrote:

The most common movements of man he has patiently plied with the why, the wherefore and the how theory. As a genius of expedients and makeshifts he can have few rivals, combining as he does something of the cunning of a savage with the practical knowledge of an engineer.

14

It was these qualities which enabled him to design an advanced ski and a new type of metal binding he later named after Lilienfeld, a village near Habernreith in Austria, which became his mountain hermitage. Here he taught a motley rabble how to ski S-turns, attributing his success to 'iron discipline which recognises no distinction of sex, age or rank'. 'It is', he wrote, 'the most primitive rule of conduct, that of two people who have dealings with each other one must be the speaker and the other the listener.' Those who listened became pupils of the world's first recognised ski school.

Just as Zdarsky had been enthused by the exploits of Nansen, his own pioneering spirit was to rub off on many others, notable amongst them his German disciple W.R. Rickmers and a kindred Austrian,

Zdarsky, who once challenged the Norwegians to a race from the summit of Mont Blanc, had cleverly adapted the lowlanders' technique to that of the mountains. And although his Lilienfeld style soon disappeared – 'the single stick', he explained, 'must never be used as a support but rather as an instrument to grope or feel with' – his name is rightly remembered as the father of Alpine skiing. In World War I he was to serve as a skiing instructor in the Austrian army and survived, with about eighty fractures and half a dozen dislocations of the spine, what Arnold Lunn once described as 'the most fearful avalanche accident that any man has come through alive'.

Schoolchildren at the turn of the century started skiing on barrel staves.

Sir Arnold Lunn.

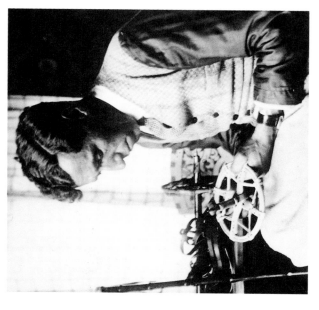

Zdarsky's eminent pupil, Hannes Schneider.

Skiers, 1930.

Hannes Schneider. Rickmers had set up a ski school at Adelboden in Switzerland where he spent several seasons instructing the British, one of who was the young Arnold Lunn.

In R.D. Blackmore's book, *Lorna Doone*, it is mentioned that skis were used in the English county of Devon over 350 years ago, but early British visitors to Switzerland had no thoughts of sampling the Alps in winter, preferring the warm summer months when perhaps they could do a little gentle hill walking or take the waters of a health-giving spa. At the end of the nineteenth century, despite the development of the transcontinental railway system, travelling through Europe was still a considerable undertaking, and it was only because of the enthusiasm of such men as Johannes Badrutt, already mentioned, and later Sir Henry Lunn, Arnold Lunn's father, who happened to run a travel business, that winter sports holidays finally became popular – initially with the British and then with the redoubtable Dutch. At first skating was all the rage, as were curling and the more adventurous sport of lugeing. Skiing therefore took very much second place, skiers being regarded mostly as figures of fun. In about

1898 one of Sir Henry's clients, Arnold relates, asked a mountain guide in Chamonix if it was possible to turn on skis. 'No', he replied, 'but it is just possible to drag yourself around on your ski-pole if you have to.'

Although a British ski club had been founded at Davos in 1903 and the first Swiss ski club at Glarus some ten years earlier, it was not until the 1920s that Alpine skiing and ski-racing really started to make an impact in the growing world of winter sports. In 1913 Arnold Lunn had proposed in his book *Skiing* that stick riding should be banned from all downhill events and it was not long before the single pole, long discarded by the British or 'Caulfield School', as it was called, disappeared from the scene. By 1922 Lunn also considered that style was playing too great a part in competitive skiing and on the occasion of the third Alpine Ski Challenge Cup, held at Mürren in Switzerland, he set an entirely new type of course, naming it a slalom, which would test speed and speed alone. It was the start of competitive Alpine skiing as we know it today, and in 1927 he visited St Anton in Austria and passed back the idea to Zdarsky's now eminent former pupil, Hannes Schneider.

THE LOVE OF SKIING

Hannes Schneider was born in the Arlberg district of Austria in 1890 and by the age of ten was infatuated with the idea of sliding down the mountains on planks. Initially, he tried his luck on barrel staves, mainly after dark when he could avoid the snowballs hurled by other children, but in 1903 was given a real pair of skis and a number of lessons on how to use them. He would watch the few early pioneers on his native slopes completing desperate turns like contortionists and slowly he began to perfect his own purer method of skiing. The more he practised the stem-christiania, as advocated by his Austrian mentor, Mathias Zdarsky, the more he began to link each turn together, and thus he became the first true exponent of the now famous Arlberg technique.

Schneider was called to St Anton as a ski instructor in 1907 and cast aside the Scandinavian telemark in favour of the christiania. As he put it 'I accustomed myself to a lower position with *vorlage* rather than the upright posture, and taught my pupils in a manner which I soon found was absolutely brilliant'. Due to Schneider, '*Kniee buegen!*' or bending and pressing the knees forward, otherwise described as *vorlage*, soon became a familiar cry in the high mountains and when in 1920, after an uncomfortable war serving on the Russian front, he produced his splendid film *Das Wunder des Schneeschuhs*, the world began a love affair with skiing which has grown from strength to strength.

Opposite: 'Of all sports skiing is the most magnificent', wrote Fridtjof Nansen in 1890. 'I know of nothing better for hardening the muscles and making the body strong and supple, for developing the qualities of resourcefulness and dexterity, and for strengthening the will or invigorating the mind. Is there anything more exhilarating or delightful on a fresh winter day than to don your skis and set off for the hills? . . . Where will you find more freedom and excitement than in speeding, as swift as a bird, down the tree-clad slopes, winter air and spruce branches rushing past your face and eyes, brain and muscles alert, ready to avoid the unknown obstacles which at any moment may be thrown in your path? It is as if all civilisation were suddenly washed from your mind and left, with the smokey atmosphere, far behind. You become one with your skis and with nature. Skiing is something which develops not only in the body, but also in the soul, and it is of the greatest importance.'

'Kristiania' (*tempera by Alfons Walde, Kitzbühel, 1925*).

THE FROZEN CONTINENT

Beyond this flood a frozen continent
Lies dark and wilde, beat with perpetual storms
Of whirlwind and dire hail, which on firm land
Thaws not, but gathers heap, and ruin seems
Of ancient pile; all else deep snow and ice.

MILTON: 'PARADISE LOST'

Fridtjof Nansen was born near Oslo in 1861 and was skiing from the time he could walk. By the age of twenty he was competing in local ski-jumping events with limited success, but there was no doubt in his mind that greater opportunities for skiing lay ahead.

In 1867 Edward Whymper, who two years earlier had achieved the first ascent of the Matterhorn, had made an abortive attempt to explore the interior of Greenland. He had been followed in 1870 and 1883 by the Swedish explorer, Adolf Nordenskiold, who, far from finding paradise, had discovered endless snow-fields on which, as Nansen later relates, 'his Lapps were said to have covered on their skis an extraordinary long distance in an astonishingly short time'.

Fired by this information, and accompanied by three Norwegians and two Lapps, early in 1888 Nansen set sail from Bergen for the icy shores of Greenland. They left the east coast in mid August 1888, climbed an exhausting 9,000ft (2,750m) and, after forty days, reached the western side in late September, returning home the following spring to a tumultuous welcome.

Nansen in his book about his exploits, *Paa Ski Over Grönland*, published in 1890, wrote an entire chapter about the art of skiing, and his many readers, who out-side Scandinavia then knew little about the subject, became immediately infatuated. It marked the dawn of skiing in the rest of the world.

Opposite: 'Everything seemed to point to the conclusion that we had reached the high plateau of the interior . . . Sanguine as we were, we hoped soon to reach the westward slope, when it would all be downward travelling and pure delight.'

Fridtjof Nansen, 1861–1930

Members of Nansen's first expedition to Greenland, 1888. Nansen (centre left) led a second expedition to Greenland in 1893. In 1922 Nansen received the Nobel Peace Prize.

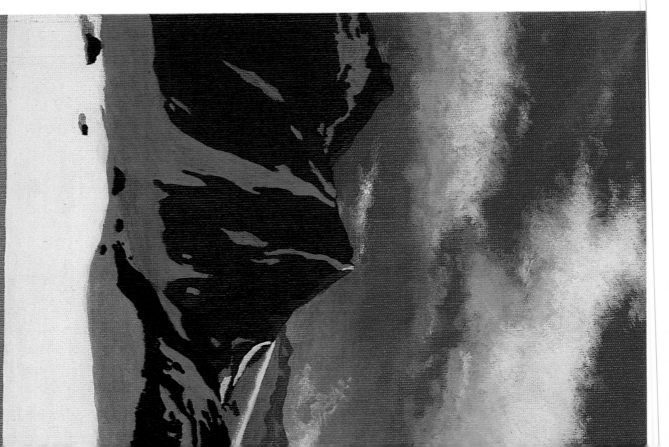

THE FIRST SKI CLUBS

News travels fast, especially on skis. Or so it seemed when not the British nor the Swiss, nor the Austrians formed the first ski club but, surprisingly, the Australians, at Kiandra in 1861, just about as far away as possible from where it all began.

As in America, it was wandering Scandinavians who introduced skis to Australia, first seen during the wild Gold Rush days of the late 1800s in the Mount Kosciusko region of New South Wales. Rising to over 7,000ft (2,135m), Australia's highest mountain is at the centre of many hundreds of square miles of Alpine terrain stretching from Canberra in the north to Melbourne in the south. The snow may lie here right through from June until the end of November and it was, and still is, the perfect playground for skiers from the southern hemisphere and for visitors from the northern hemisphere who enjoy their skiing the whole year round. Many of the early adventurers arrived from the bush with skis tied to the saddles of their horses, and when the Kiandra Snow Shoe Club opened their bar, the Aussie thirst for living it up in the mountains became unquenchable. In 1898, the New South Wales Alpine Club, later to be merged with the Kosciusko Alpine Club, was formed, and arguably became the fourth ski club in the world.

Apart from that at Kiandra, the earliest ski clubs were those founded at La Porte in California in 1867, and at Christiania, now Oslo, in 1877. 'In California's "Lost Sierras"', wrote Big Bill Berry from Nevada, 'Gold-Rush miners fostered the birth of American skiing . . . and cradled it into such an inherent part of their lives that they established what is thought to be the first organised ski competition the world has known.' In 1887 the CSK Praha, in Czechoslovakia, then called Bohemia, became the first ski club in Central Europe, and a year later Sir Arthur Conan Doyle, creator of Sherlock Holmes, by crossing the Swiss Alps on skis from Davos to Arosa, helped to encourage the formation of the first British ski club at Davos in 1901. By the turn of the century ski competitions were gaining such popularity that clubs such as the Ski Club of Great Britain, inaugurated in the Cafe Royale in London in 1903, far away from any snowfields, were soon an integral part of the winter sporting scene.

Mail arriving at Kiandra, 1870.

Two jolly swagmen, Australia, 1960s.

August in the southern hemisphere is the equivalent of February in the Swiss Alps and is usually glorious. I was fortunate to ski at Portillo (above) in Chile one summer where there are runs descending for over 3,500ft (1,066m) on the slopes of Aconcagua, the highest mountain in the Andes. I shared a huge barbecued steak at the top of the ski-lift with a hefty Argentinian fellow and we raced each other down for the favours of a pretty fur-wrapped Venezuelan girl, who sadly declined to watch us. Probably she did not understand, I consoled myself, that such duels had been held there since skiing first started in 1890, although the Chilean Ski Club, formed in 1930, probably would have frowned. There are several other excellent ski resorts in South America, some with organised heliskiing, Bariloche, in Argentina, being one of the best known.

AUTHOR'S COMMENT.

Opposite: Skiing 'down under' among the snow-gums in the Snowy Mountains. In the good old mining days, downhill races at Kiandra were known as the 'flying furlong' and cross-country events as 'lung-busters'.

DOWNHILL ONLY

The world's first downhill race, for a cup presented by Lord Roberts of Kandahar, a British general, was held at Montana, Switzerland, in 1911. The Kandahar Ski Club, which was to revolutionise competitive skiing, was founded by Arnold Lunn at Mürren, Switzerland, in January 1924. In the same year the *Fédération Internationale de Ski* (FIS) was formed and the first Winter Olympic Games were held in Chamonix. Lunn, who was seldom lost for words, described his new form of competition in these terms:

Neither the Swedish president of the FIS, nor the Norwegian vice-president, could have envisaged a future in which the main interest at the Olympic Games would be focused not on Langlauf and Jumping [as had been the case in competitions previously], but on Downhill and a new form of competition [the slalom] invented by an Englishman [himself] of whom they had never heard, at a Swiss centre they had never visited.

The Kandahar Ski Club, named after a town in Afghanistan where nobody skied, was bound to provoke rivalry, and in the following year the Downhill Only Club (DHO) was founded at Wengen with the principal objective of avenging a previous defeat by the Kandahar, which they fortunately managed to do in nil visibility the following season. Dr Zahnd, Kur-direktor of Wengen at the time, writing about a further occasion said:

The team race between the DHO and the local skiers gave the Wengeners their first incentive to master the alpine forms of competition and at last the job of learning to ski seriously . . . the English provided a *Sportliches Vorbild* (sporting model) in the best sense of the word, for the Wengeners learned from them not only to race and do battle but also to lose.

President of the Wengen Ski Club at that time was Ernst Gertsch, who some years later conceived a down-hill course, the Lauberhorn, which is still one of the best known in the world. In 1928 Lunn and Hannes Schneider staged the first Arlberg–Kandahar, which was to become the 'blue ribbon' of downhill racing.

Downhill courses today are usually set over a distance of about 2 miles (3.2km) with a drop of up to 3,300ft (1,000m) for men and 2,300ft (700m) for women and take around two minutes to complete. Reaching speeds of up to 90mph (144kph) with an average speed of often more than 60mph (97kph), the competitors must not only show great courage and determination, but have immense reserves of stamina and superb technique.

Note: The DHO club was formed by Dick Waghorn, winner of the 1929 Schneider Trophy air race in the famous Supermarine S6.

Above right: Toni Sailer, Austria. Winner of all three gold medals in the 1956 Olympics, and winner of the giant slalom, downhill and combined titles in both the 1956 and 1958 World Championships. In 1956 he also won the slalom.

Centre right: Franz Klammer, Austria. Winner of the World Cup downhill title in 1975, 1976, 1977, 1978 and amazingly five years later in 1983. Popular winner of the downhill gold medal at the 1976 Olympic Games in Innsbruck.

Right: Pirmin Zurbriggen, Switzerland. Winner of the World Cup downhill title in 1985, 1987 and 1988. His list of victories in World Cup races is substantial and in 1988 he achieved his ambition of winning the Olympic downhill at Calgary.

Damit dem Fahrer nichts passiert,
Ist seine Route klar markiert
Drum zugle Deiner Bretter Schwung
Gefährlich ist ein — Seitensprung.

Opposite: Pirmin Zurbriggen (Zubie) of Switzerland, downhill gold medal winner, flying down Mount Allan at the 1988 Olympics in Calgary. In 1987 he equalled Jean-Claude Killy's long-standing record by winning four World Cup titles in the same season.

FLYING LADIES

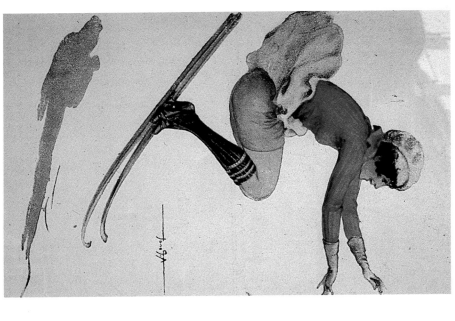

Alice Damrosch Wolfe, who managed the first American women's team in 1935, in Roland Palmedo's book, *Skiing, the International Sport*, wrote:

In Mürren the Kandahar Club was developing an extraordinarily fine group of girl racers. They were the first girls to have esprit-de-corps, courage and grit. Also, thanks to Mr Arnold Lunn, they were the first girls to have a formal training . . . It was English girls to have a formal training . . . It was English girls at the 1929 races at Zakopane, Poland, and at St Anton-am-Arlberg, Austria, who first put racing for women on the map. What a flutter they caused in central Europe! . . . Their long straight legs encased, sometimes, in even longer beautifully tailored, flapping dark blue trousers, caused the most openmouthed wonder and astonishment, and when these slim creatures could also ski, it was really too much!

As the years went by, Austrian maids from the mountains began to overhaul the English girls and in 1934 a German lady, Christel Cranz, took over, and by winning five World Championships and the Olympic gold medal for the combined in 1936, secured her position as the greatest woman racer of all time. The legendary Austrian skier Annemarie Moser-Proell came close to challenging her in the late 1970s and latterly the accomplished Swiss skier Vreni Schneider, but in the beauty stakes Maria Walliser, also of Switzerland and winner of the World Cup title in 1985 and 1987, must surely win hands down.

'What a flutter they caused . . .'

Baronin Gratia Schimmelpenninsk van der Oye from Holland, competing at Arosa, Switzerland, in 1938.

Opposite: A flying lady.

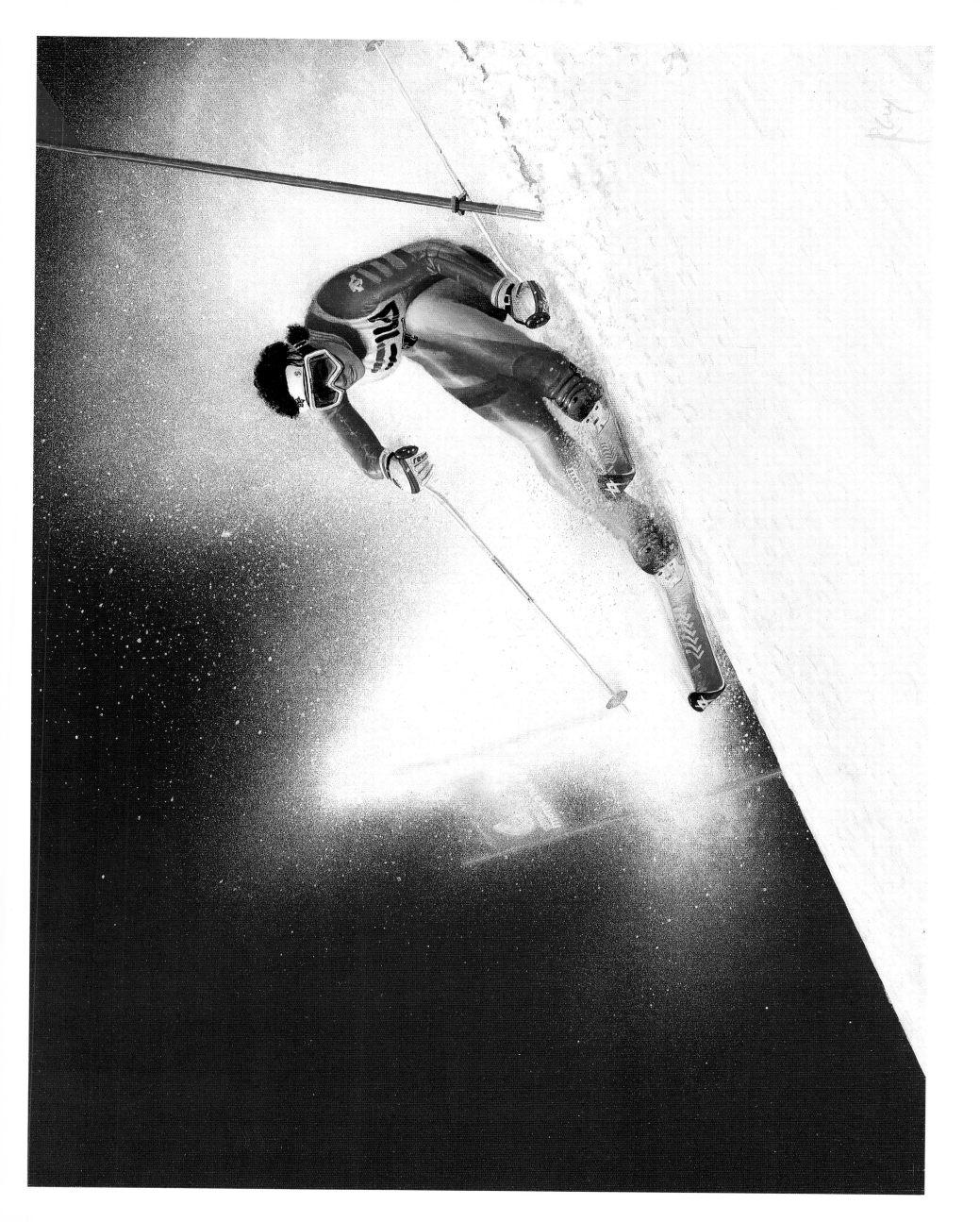

GIANT SLALOM

In 1905 the Austrian, Mathias Zdarsky, who had pioneered techniques for skiing in steep mountain terrain, organised the first slalom race in skiing history on the slopes of Muckenkogel, near the hamlet of Lilienfeld, in lower Austria. In many ways the course resembled, with flags and not yet gates, the giant slalom courses of today.

One of the greatest giant slalom racers ever was Toni Sailer of Austria. Over four years of his career, from 1955 to 1958, he did not lose a single major giant slalom, often winning by impressive margins. Sailer's secret in the giant slalom was his ability to carve smooth edgeless turns. The American Phil Mahre also perfected this technique several years later and became master of the modern super giant slalom as well. Phil Mahre and his twin brother Steve were the most

successful skiers that America has ever produced. In 1980 Phil won the Alpine combination at the Winter Olympics in Lake Placid. The following year Phil, master of the giant slalom, had the best overall placing in the World Cup, as he did in 1982 when he won both the slalom and the giant slalom, beating the redoubtable Swede, Ingemar Stenmark, with whom he eventually duelled for five nail-biting years. Not to be outdone, Steve won the Olympic giant slalom the same season.

Opposite: In 1983 Phil Mahre repeated his win in the 1982 World Cup giant slalom (depicted here) and once more had the best overall placing. His astonishing success story will be hard for any non European to beat.

Slalom courses in the early part of the century were set between small flags.

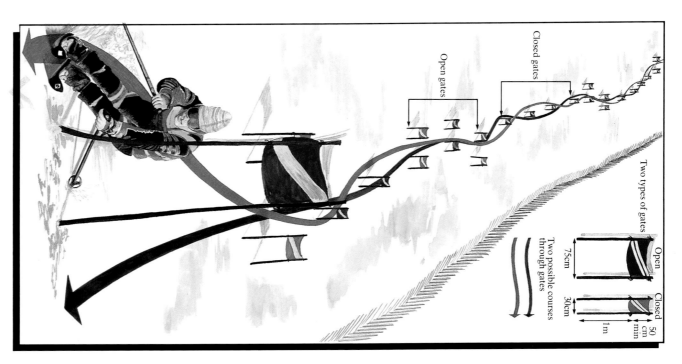

Giant slalom, first conceived at Planica in Yugoslavia, was designed to combine much of the excitement and dash of the downhill with the controlled skills of the slalom. The racer is tested at pre-jumping, tucking, skating, riding bumps and executing smooth accelerating turns – all at high speed. Giant slalom was regarded as just another event until it was included in the 1950 World Championships and the 1952 Winter Olympic Games. The gates in giant slalom resemble those used in downhill, only they are placed much closer together. Not less than 35 gates must be set on the men's courses which are between 985ft and 1,659ft (300m and 500m) in length, and 30 gates on ladies' courses which are between 985ft and 1,475ft (300m and 450m) in length. The super giant slalom, which first appeared in the 1982 World Cup, is longer and often steeper.

Two types of gates

Two possible courses through gates

Closed gates

Open gates

Open | Closed

75cm | 30cm

1m

50 cm | 1 mm

WINTER OLYMPIC GAMES

The Italian contingent at the 1928 Olympics held in St Moritz, Switzerland.

Tony Nash, bob driver, and Robin Dixon, brakeman, winners of one of Great Britain's few Winter Olympic gold medals, at Innsbruck, Austria, 1964. (The author helped search the ice for Nash's contact lenses before the final run, but without success. It obviously pays to go down the bob run with your eyes shut!) (*Oil painting by Roy Nockolds*)

From 1901 the Nordic Games had been held every four years at Holmenkollen, Norway, and included cross-country competitions, Bandy, a Nordic form of ice hockey and, naturally, ski jumping. The Games had rapidly become an institution and, as Arnold Lunn wrote later when comparing the event to the Summer Olympics:

I myself felt that there was something which, for want of a more accurate description, could only be described as a mystique about Holmenkollen and which recalled the classic Olympics, restricted as Herodotus wrote, 'to those who had common temples and sacrifices and like ways of life'.

After 1911, when Alpine skiing began to come into its own, thanks largely to Lunn himself, and subsequent to figure skating being included in the London Olympics of 1908, there was a growing movement to hold an entirely separate winter games. At first many of those on the Olympic committee refused to throw off the Nordic connection and continued to resist; but after ice hockey had been added to the Antwerp Games in 1920 and a successful Winter Sports Week had been held in Chamonix, France, in 1924 – which also included ski jumping, cross-country skiing and

bobsleigh – Chamonix was retrospectively awarded the honour of having held the first Winter Olympic Games. When slalom was added at Garmisch-Partenkirchen in 1936, 60,000 spectators watched the event. Alpine skiing, however, was still not accepted as an Olympic sport until the 1948 Olympics at St Moritz.

In 1952 the Games, in deference to the Nordic lobby, were held in Oslo, the homeland of skiing. Downhill and slalom had by now become so popular that twenty-seven countries entered for the events, but the bias remained, and interest concentrated on the Nordic combination of cross-country and jumping almost to the exclusion of the two new races. Matters were not finally put right until the 1956 Olympics at Cortina d'Ampezzo, Italy, when the great Austrian skier Toni Sailer hit the headlines by winning all three Alpine gold medals. Since then – in 1960 at Squaw Valley, USA; in 1964 at Innsbruck, Austria; in 1968 at Grenoble, France; in 1972 at Sapporo, Japan; in 1976 at Innsbruck again; in 1980 at Lake Placid, USA; in 1984 at Sarajevo, Yugoslavia and in 1988 at Calgary, Canada – Olympic Alpine events have never looked back.

The legendary Jean-Claude Killy of France, winner of all three gold medals and the Alpine Combined title at the 1968 Olympics held at Grenoble in France.

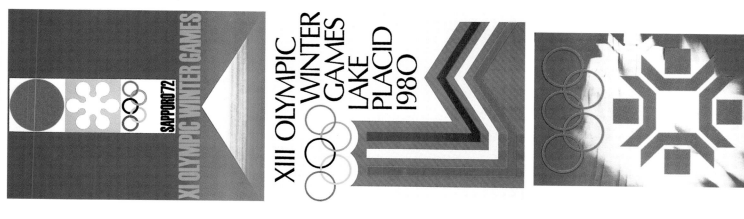

Franz Klammer, Austria, who in his famous yellow racing suit became a world hero after winning the gold medal for the downhill at the 1976 Winter Olympics in Innsbruck. 'I ski only against the mountain, never against the man', he once remarked during an astonishing career which included an unprecedented twenty-five victories in the World Cup.

SPECIAL SLALOM

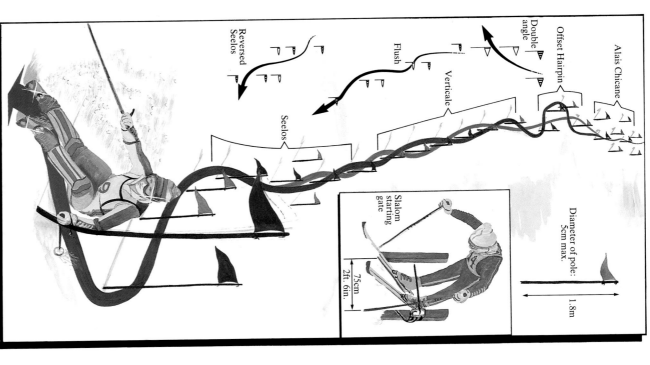

Slalom is a sabre dance, not performed with swords to a crescendo of thrilling music, but with flashing skis through a chorus of yelling supporters. Good slalom skiers are artists, able to turn through a maze of gates accurately, smoothly and at high speed.

The concept of the slalom may well have started in the forests of Scandinavia but, as an event, it was the brainchild of the father of Alpine ski-racing, Sir Arnold Lunn. In 1921 competitors in the first British Ski Championship had been asked to complete a series of turns on which they were judged for style; but inevitably, because speed and dash were discouraged, the event had fallen on its face. Lunn, being at that time in possession of a small silver trophy destined for a golf match, decided instead to present it for a new type of ski race. Competitors were given additional points for speed, marking for style was dropped, and his Alpine Ski Challenge Cup, first held at Mürren in Switzerland, became a pure slalom race and the blueprint for slaloms of the future. Falling was originally part of the game, for competitors found it far quicker to throw themselves down between the poles, turning as they fell, than take a more prudent line. For several years therefore, until standards improved, a ten-second penalty had to be imposed for each fall. By 1930, however, courses were being set on hard-packed snow with start numbers dictated by placings in the downhill, which was always held first. Only one timed run on each of two different courses counted, and the early start numbers were reversed for the second descent.

In 1966, in the Andes, the World Cup was born and with it the era of televised skiing and stars such as Jean-Claude Killy. The courses are much the same now except for one major difference, the flexible 'rapid gate'.

Since the introduction of articulated poles, slalom has required more bravado than ever. Today's slalomer must train by punching through thousands of gates and endure constant bruising – a far cry from Arnold Lunn's original idea of penalising those who knocked ping-pong balls off the top of the poles. Slaloms are raced against the clock and the winner has the best aggregate time over two runs. Gates are made from self-righting plastic poles and are placed in alternate colours in a regulated number of recognised combinations which test a racer's skill and judgement to the limit. Although the poles appear to be placed haphazardly they must not interrupt a racer's fluency. The vertical drop of each course should be a minimum 600ft (180m) for men and 425ft (130m) for women, and the minimum number of gates differs from 55 to 45 accordingly.

Stein Erikson of Norway, winner of the giant slalom and second in the slalom in the 1952 Olympics, won both slalom titles in the 1954 World Championships. Always popular, he did much to pass on his technique to others.

Ingemar Stenmark of Sweden, winner of the Olympic gold medals for slalom and giant slalom in 1980 and the World Cup slalom from 1975–81 and in 1983. Stenmark was equally successful in the World Cup giant slalom.

Tomba, 'la Bomba', of Italy, a slalomer of purpose. Winner of two gold medals – for slalom and giant slalom – at the 1988 Olympics, and the World Cup slalom title in 1988 by winning no less than nine World Cup races.

Opposite: Ingemar Stenmark, famous for his second-run 'charge', came from the new school, and is acknowledged as the greatest slalom specialist the world has seen. When he retired in March 1989 he had achieved 86 World Cup wins in slalom and giant slalom over a 16-year career. He is shown here racing before the advent of flexible poles.

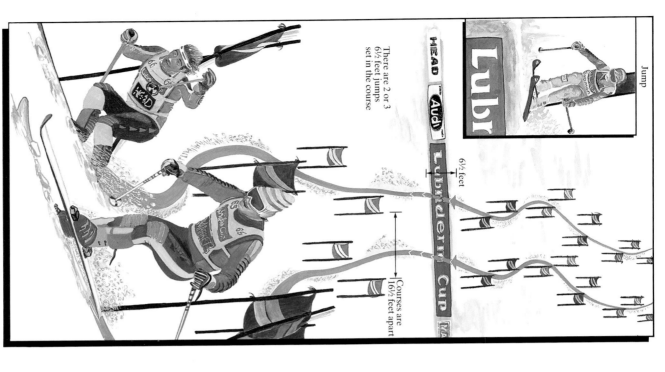

Jump

There are 2 or 3 6½ feet jumps set in the course

6½ feet

Courses are 16½ feet apart

THE PROFESSIONALS

Many of the best instructors in the early days of Alpine skiing travelled the world as ambassadors of the new sport. It was largely due to them that skiing gained such universal popularity between the two world wars.

Most professional amongst them was Hannes Schneider, the guru of the Arlberg technique, who in 1930 left his native Austria first for America and then for a protracted training session in Japan. The Japanese are built for skiing and Schneider found that he could teach them his turns without difficulty. They seemed to bounce down the mountain like rubber balls and were more determined to master his method than any other students he had previously instructed.

Ski school for the Japanese had started in 1911 when Major Theodore von Lerch, military attaché to the Austrian Embassy in Tokyo, came to Takada city, north of the main island, and taught skiing to a special group of ten army officers. In 1925 the National Ski Association of Japan (SAJ) was founded with the intention of promoting skiing as a national sport, and since then Japan has produced some notable champions such as Chiharu Igaya, winner of the silver medal for slalom in the 1956 Olympics at Cortina d'Ampezzo, Italy. In 1972 the Winter Olympics were held at Sapporo, Japan, and today the country, which in its northern regions may sometimes have snow as deep as 15ft (5m), plays an increasingly important role on the World Cup circuit.

The SAJ now employs a large staff managing some 25,000 professional ski instructors. All are necessary, for from mid December to the end of April the mountains of Japan may echo to the sound of no less than 15 million Japanese skiers.

When Karl Schranz, Olympic gold medallist and the greatest downhiller of his day, returned to Vienna, Austria, having been banned from the Winter Olympic Games at Sapporo, Japan, in 1972 by the International Olympic Committee, he was welcomed home by 100,000 of his countrymen. His crime was that he had earned money from skiing which had not been channelled through his national ski federation, considered 'the done thing' on the world professional skiing circuit. Pro Championships, first held in January 1961 on Buttermilk Mountain, Colorado, USA, and now sponsored by large companies for substantial prizes, include freestyle competitions and a thrilling parallel slalom. Professional ski racing was confined almost exclusively to North America until, in March 1988, the Fujitsu World Pro Ski Festival was held at Sapporo.

初級 EASY

上級 DIFFICULT

中級 MODERATE

JAPANESE SKI SIGNS

Hannes Schneider in America, on his way to Japan, January 1930.

Chiharu Igaya airborne. A far greater percentage of Japanese enjoy Alpine skiing than that of any other people in the world.

Opposite: Japanese ski instructors tackle the moguls at the time of the eleventh Interski Congress at Zoah, Japan, in 1979.

An early display of ballet, 1931.

If slalom courses were first devised to simulate a head-long plunge through a dense forest of trees, bone-shattering mogul bashing is a sport which could only have been thought up, one surmises, by those who have taken far too much sun in a desert dune-buggy. Yet as the hard-beaten snow of the piste is inevitably shaped into hummocks by an ever-increasing volume of skiers, a technique has evolved on how to manage this unevenness. The early exponents of the Arlberg school are no more likely to have experienced moguls than the mink-gloved followers of the latest snow-grooming machines, yet it was they who were initially responsible for the sheep-like following that carves the piste into icy monuments. Competitors in modern freestyle events, however, could hardly do without those hummocks.

Competitors will normally attempt one or more of three freestyle events – moguls, ballet and aerials – before a panel of eight judges. In the mogul event judges base their scores on a combination of skill and raw aggression. Points are awarded for speed on the fall line, rhythm, the number of turns accomplished, for at least two upright jumps and for the most sensational airborne manoeuvres completed. All this on a 65ft (20m) wide strip of the steepest, bumpiest and nastiest stretch of piste that can be found.

Ballet is only less demanding because it is held on a more gentle slope. Each competitor performs a choreographed routine for 2.25 minutes and each, similar to figure skaters, must include a variety of spins, multi-rotational jumps, dance-like steps and flips over parallel poles to somehow achieve a score for gracefulness.

In contrast to ballet, the aerial competition takes everyone's breath away, not least the competitors'. The tracks, like ski jumps, descend steeply to a number

of different launch pads and a landing zone much resembling the side of a house. Points are scored on the height and distance achieved for two different jumps either in an upright or inverted position. The sum of the judges' marks is then multiplied by a 'degree of difficulty' factor which leaves most computers smoking!

'Hot dogging'. In the mogul event points are awarded 25% for speed, 25% for jumps and 50% for technique.

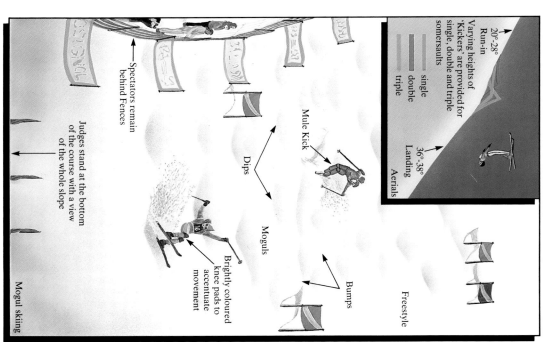

Opposite: Can the 'Red Arrows' do any better? In the aerial event points are awarded 20% for height, 50% for the form of jump and 30% for the landing.

Axel Henriksen, an early devotee, turns a complete somersault on skis at Duluth, Minnesota, USA, in 1913. But freestyle is the youngest Alpine discipline to be recognised as an international winter sport, confirmed when the first every Freestyle World Championships were held at Tignes, France, in 1986. Two Canadians, in the aerials and combined events, became world champions, and when the Winter Olympics were held in Calgary in 1988, freestyle skiing, still dominated by Canadians, was demonstrated as a possible future Olympic competition.

ONE SKI WILL DO

The birth of skiing in New Zealand

It is likely that the first skis used in New Zealand were carried there by Norwegian miners working in the Serpentine goldfields of Central Otago in about 1874. The mountains there, in the Rough Ridge Range, were under snow for several months of the year and skis seemed simply the most practical method of transport. Not until 1893, however, were skis used in New Zealand's Southern Alps when three stalwart gentlemen, Dixon, Mannering and Fyfe, made what Dixon described as 'the first Siege of Mount Cook'. They had decided on the attempt after reading Nansen's book *Paa Ski Over Grönland* and although skis were not then readily available, as Mannering wrote later:

Dixon, with his customary ingenuity, conceived the idea of utilising the fans off a corn reaper, which are shaped very much like skis and turn up at either end and I fancy are made of hickory . . . We found them an enormous advantage in crossing the Great Plateau and on the Linda Glacier. They saved hours of sounding for covered crevasses and almost banished the constant anxiety which accompanies such work.

The first New Zealand ski club was formed in 1913 at Ruapehu and the first Alpine championships, known as the Aorangi Ski Championships, were held in the Mount Cook region in 1931. Today from July to October many skiers visit New Zealand, particularly from neighbouring Australia.

For those who do not wish to spend too much time inverted on skis, there is another way. The 'monomaniac', a species discovered in the French Alps and first acknowledged by the ski school at Les Arcs in 1982, is the closest thing to the yeti, that elusive Himalayan mammal, that has ever graced the mountains. Many a skier has wondered at the wandering tracks that now so often thread down in dotted lines through rocky labyrinths where only a madman dare go; they create a whole new sign language—one that can be truly understood only by acute sufferers of this new form of ski fever.

'Single-plankers' can now choose between a straight monoski on which the skier faces forwards with his feet in parallel bindings, or the wider snowboard, which has bindings facing almost at right angles to the direction of flight. There are enthusiasts for both varieties, the one giving an impression of skiing with the feet tied together and the other to windsurfing on a sea of concrete — or so it would seem until one carves one's way off the piste into the powder and the better side of heaven. No wonder that monoskiing is now part of the curriculum of any decent ski school, and that beginners are already asking the question 'Why learn on two skis when one ski will do?'.

Possibly the first 'monomaniac', Austria, 1930.

A ski surfer.

Opposite: Surf skiing on a volcano – anything is possible in New Zealand.

TAKING IT STRAIGHT

'Although there is no wind, very soon the chattering of the skis is lost to the howling crescendo in your ears as the noise erupts to an emotive thunderous roar – like Concorde breaking the sound barrier. Trying to maintain a tight tuck position becomes almost impossible as the immense pressure forces you upwards and backwards, trying to rip you apart.' Words of a brave man, Stuart Wilkie, whose brother Graham in 1987 set the world ski speed record of just over 132mph (212kph), a remarkable feat for any lowlander.

So great is the urge to break the 150mph (240kph) barrier, that only five months later a Frenchman, Michael Prufer, smoked down a 45 degree avalanche chute (about the steepest slope on which snow will hold) at Portillo in Chile to achieve a new record of 135mph (217kph). Prufer, a doctor who competes for Monaco, described how his pulse was racing at 200 beats a minute before he jumped off. He then accelerated to over 60mph (100kph) in just 3 seconds, faster than a Formula One racing car, and descended quicker than a free-fall parachutist to find an inner peace as his skis started to glide and his pulse rate dropped off to well below normal. Not so the pulses of the blurred crowd of spectators below, for they know all about the damaging burns that can be inflicted at these speeds should the racer fall (the author once burned through three sweaters when falling near the finish of the Cresta toboggan run) and how quickly a polyurethan-coated Lycra skin suit can be blown to pieces should the racer 'chicken' and try to stand up!

There had been a competition, known as the *Kilometro Lanciato*, at Cervinia in Italy since the early 1920s; but well before then several men had made determined attempts to become the fastest in the world on skis. As early as 1863 on the 'Big Hill' at Onion Valley in California, an American, William Metcalf, established an unofficial world record of 71.5mph (115kph); and six years later in Plumas County, California, an unofficial record was set of 87mph (140kph) which was not to be beaten until Zeno Colo of Italy took the record to 98.8mph (159.3kph) in May 1948. It is unlikely that speed skiers, such as the Wilkie brothers, will allow so much time to elapse between records again.

In March 1987 Emmanuel (Manu) Bellier, an instructor at the ski school in Val d'Isère, France, established a new world record for monoski of 112mph (180.2kph).

Old-time speedster.

One way to achieve the record.

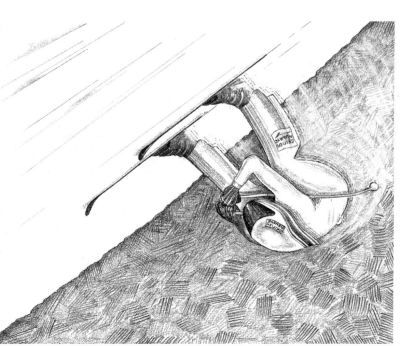

The equipment used by today's speed merchant has usually been wind-tunnel tested or tried out with the skier strapped to the roof of a car travelling at up to 140mph (225kph). Skis must not now exceed 8ft (2.5m) in length.

Although carefully weighted skis with handholds had been used on a previous attempt, the Italian racer Zeno Colo established a new world record in 1948 using no special equipment whatsoever.

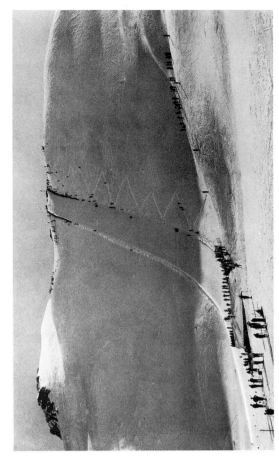

The 'Flying Kilometre' at St Moritz was set up in January 1930 by a young Swiss protégé of Arnold Lunn, Walter Amstutz, and was the first such course to have precision timing. Amstutz, who later founded the famous Schweizerischer Akademischer Ski Club (SAS), became the most respected Swiss pioneer of Alpine ski-racing.

Ice chute at La Clusaz, on the World Cup speed skiing circuit, in France. After an approximate 1,000ft (305m) run in on well-packed snow, speed skiers are clocked over a 300ft (100m) time trap (the 'Flying Kilometre' was always a misnomer), before braking hard on an inclined slope.

NORDIC SKING

Skiing, a way of life in Norway.

Ice hockey, which was recognised as a Winter Olympic sport at the 1920 Games in Antwerp, also originated from Scandinavia.

FINMARKEN

damstett

'There are three lines running through Norwegian history,' a patriot wrote in 1903. 'One is the furrow scored by the peasant's ploughshare; the second, the wakes of our ships across the seven seas; the third, the ski tracks that girdle the earth.'

The earliest report (unconfirmed) of ski-racing in Norway is of a contest between Heming Aslaksen (the Norwegian William Tell) and his king during the first century AD. According to the book *De Gentibus Septentrionalibus*, published by the Swedish archbishop Olaus Magnus in 1555, the Lapps were racing for silver and other prizes from early in the second century. However the first confirmed race in ski history was held at Tromsö, northern Norway, in 1843 and this surprisingly included *langlauf* (cross-country), jumping and a downhill. The downhill event was soon to be dropped, however, and until 1930 the Holmenkollen competition, first held just outside Oslo in 1892 and consisting solely of *langlauf* and jumping, remained the standard event for all Scandinavians. Norway neglected the downhill more and more, and when the sport of skiing spread into Central Europe at the end of the nineteenth century the strong Norwegian influence remained against downhill races, so that most competitions continued with the two disciplines, cross-country and jumping, alone.

It was not however until after the first downhill race in the Alps, the Roberts of Kandahar, had been held at Montana, Switzerland, in 1911 that the Nordic/Alpine split began to crack wide open.

Downhill and slalom racers were too cowardly to jump and too feeble to race cross-country, it was said by all but the British, until in 1928 the Austrians accepted the new disciplines – but only for women.

'Assume the normal position for straight running with the knees rigidly together, then drop into the telemark position by advancing the right ski if you intend to turn to the left and the left ski if you want to turn to the right. Advance the leading ski far enough for the upturn of the back ski to rest against the ankle of the front foot. Both skis should be held in contact and the knees should be bowed inwards. The front knee should be in the emphasised "forward knee" position, and the back knee should also be well bent. You are now in position to start the turn.' From *Instructions on Accomplishing the Telemark* by Arnold Lunn.

Before the christiania turn was perfected by the great Mathias Zdarsky, an Austrian who at the end of the nineteenth century adapted Nordic skiing for the steeper slopes of the Alps, the telemark, invented by Sondre Norheim and named after the Telemark region of his native Norway, was the recognised method of turning downhill.

Opposite: Telemark skiing in Norway today. Written about in a recent book, *Norway's Gift to the World*, the technique is making an important comeback with races being held in most skiing areas. There is talk of its one day becoming an Olympic event.

JUMPING FOR JOY

'The whole undertaking requires considerable daring at first, for the view from the summit of a ski jump is one calculated to alarm the novice. The danger is, however, almost purely imaginary, and a common amount of pluck will soon overcome the initial qualms.' Is this from an early treatise on ski jumping – or are they the words of Eddie ('The Eagle') Edwards the British ski jumper who got full marks for trying in the 1988 Winter Olympics?

It was probably the redoubtable Norwegian Sondre Norheim who first launched himself into space in about the year 1840, and in 1860 he is known to have jumped 100ft (30.5m). It was not until 1900 that this record was beaten. Today, in comparison, the record stands at more than six times that distance, a jump of 636ft (194m) having been made by the Pole, Piotr Fijas, at Planica in Yugoslavia, where 'ski flying' first started, during March 1987. For a long time jumping officials have felt that such an event, which is extremely dangerous in windy conditions, has been developed far enough, and it is now treated separately to the Nordic competitions and held on 230ft (70m) and 297ft (90m) jumps only.

Ski jumping is judged on both distance and style and the key to success is not, surprisingly, just bravado but superb technique, particularly on the *satz* or take-off, where the jumper must explode into the air with incredible precision and no undue wind resistance. The perfect jump is an aggressive one with the body stretched far forward, motionless, with the skis parallel, followed by a firm telemark landing but one that is also as light as a feather.

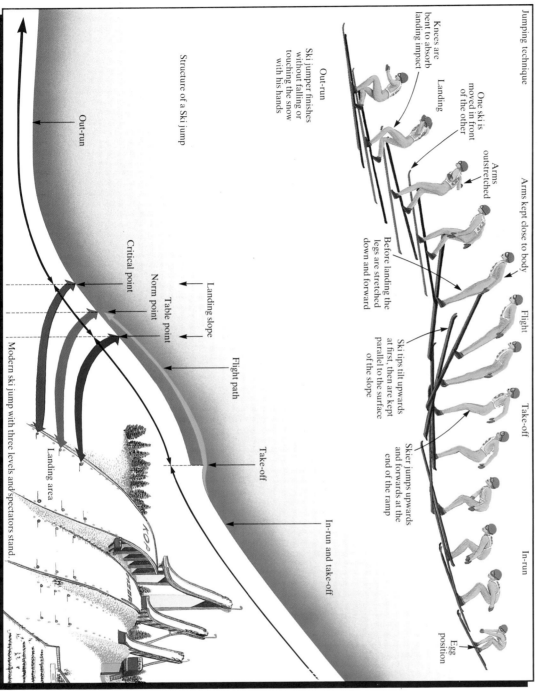

Jumping technique

- Knees are bent to absorb landing impact
- Landing
- One ski is moved in front of the other
- Arms outstretched
- Arms kept close to body
- Before landing the legs are stretched down and forward
- Flight
- Ski tips tilt upwards at first, then are kept parallel to the surface of the slope
- Take-off
- Skier jumps upwards and forwards at the end of the ramp
- In-run
- Egg position

Structure of a Ski jump

- Out-run
- Ski jumper finishes without falling or touching the snow with his hands
- Out-run
- Critical point
- Norm point
- Table point
- Landing slope
- Flight path
- Take-off
- In-run and take-off
- Landing area
- Modern ski jump with three levels and spectators stand.

A typical ski jump.

Ski jumper (*Alfons Walde, c. 1910*).

Opposite: Matti ('Nukes') Nykaenen, the 'Flying Finn', in full flight. His coach maintained that 98 per cent of Nykaenen's success was due to raw courage.

BESUCHEN SIE

PONTRESINA

ANLÄSSLICH DER WINTER-OLYMPIADE IN ST. MORITZ
FEBRUAR 1928

Matti Nykaenen, the only man to have won three Olympic gold medals for ski jumping and winner of both events at the 1988 Olympics in Calgary, is considered the greatest ski jumper of all time. 'It's like someone's filled the guy with helium', said one Canadian spectator at the Games.

CROSS-COUNTRY

At the inaugural Olympic Games held at Chamonix in 1924 there were no downhill or slalom events and only Nordic skiing was included. Ladies, however, were not allowed to compete until the 1952 Olympics in Oslo.

There were three main competitions at Chamonix, the 13 mile (18km) cross-country, or *langlauf*, race, the 31 mile (50km) race and the ski jumping. The jumping points and the 18km points were also added to give a 'Combined' result. Now the 'Nordic Combined' is a separate event altogether and is scored on the results of 230ft (70m) jumping on the first day and a 9 mile (15km) *langlauf* race on the second day.

A Norwegian, Thorleif Haug, won the first Olympic 13 mile (18km) race. He beat another Norwegian by a wide margin and then repeated his victory in the marathon, defeating his fellow countryman, Thoralf

Stroemstad, by nearly two minutes. His bronze medal in the jumping then gave him the gold for the Combined. However, in 1974, no less than fifty years later, Stroemstad, who had been examining the points again, proved to the International Olympic Committee (IOC) that the placings in the jumping at Chamonix had been incorrect. As a result Haug, who had been long since dead, was relegated to fourth position and an American, Anders Haugen, at the age of eighty-three, was awarded the bronze and America's one and only Olympic jumping medal.

Today the competition remains equally ferocious. But, unlike ski jumping, at least *langlauf*, or *ski de fond* as the French prefer to call it, continues to be a sport for the millions of skiers, both young and old, who are just out to enjoy themselves.

Exercising the dog.

Opposite: Cross-country skiing. A walk in the Black Forest.

SKATERS' WALTZ

'To feel yourself carried along with the speed of an arrow and the graceful undulations of a bird in flight, on a smooth, shining, resonant and yet treacherous surface: by a simple balancing of the body and by using your will as a rudder, to change direction like a ship at sea or like an eagle soaring in the blue sky; for me this was such an intoxication of the senses and such a voluptuous dizziness of thought that I cannot recall it without emotion. Even horses, that I have loved so much, do not give to the rider the delirium that ice gives to the skater.' (Alphonse De Lamartine, 1832)

The seeds of the sport of skating were probably first sown in Holland and the first known illustration of skating was a wood engraving in Brugman's *Vita Lydwina*, printed in 1498, depicting an unfortunate damsel who in 1396, at the tender age of sixteen, fell on the ice and broke a rib while skating. She entered a convent, where she died in 1433, and later she came to be known as St Lydwina of Schiedam, the patron saint of skaters.

The movements of arms and legs must be coordinated and rhythmic. The constant kick off with one foot, slide on the other, must synchronise with the pole strokes so that an even speed may be maintained and the work divided between arms and legs. The body must keep in a straight line and not bob up and down and the skis must be made to slide as far as possible with each step. Then all you need is a great deal of stamina to become a good cross-country skier.

Goster Olander, Norwegian professional coach

The classical cross-country style is pretty to watch yet economical in energy over considerable distances such as the world's most famous Nordic ski race, the Vasaloppet. Held to commemorate Gustav Vasa's epic journey in 1520 from Mora to Sälen in Sweden (see page 3), the race covers 55 miles (89km) and now attracts more than twelve thousand skiers. Similar ski marathons are now held in many other countries, the longest being the Grenader held near Oslo and the König Ludwig Lauf held at Oberammergau, West Germany, both only 5/8 mile (1km) further at nearly 56 miles (90km). The Canadians hold a 99 mile (160km) ski marathon from Lachute, Quebec, to Ottawa, Ontario, but it is run in stages over two days.

To the chagrin of many, particularly of Scandinavians, the classical style now has a rival. Since the early 1980s the 'skating' step, allowed because of a loophole in International Ski Federation (FIS) rules which failed to ban the new technique in World Cup competitions until 1985, has been rapidly taking hold. At the 1988 Olympics, freestyle, which in *langlauf* language means 'skating', was treated as a demonstration event, and now that classical and skating are split 50-50 in the World Cup schedule, the Olympic Committee is having to accept the new faster style as a separate discipline. But although skating is quicker it has certain drawbacks, not least the wear and tear on the skier. Dr Fred Auer, the eminent St Moritz practitioner who has seen the Engadine Marathon grow to the size of the Vasaloppet, and who has *langlaufed* most winters to his office, believes that cross-country skiing, far from being a graceful and healthy sport, is fast becoming too exacting and damaging to the health of many racers. Classical or skating step, the controversy continues, perhaps cross-country racers would be better off just dancing the 'Skater's Waltz!'

Today's racers may not find room to 'skate', even on a lake!

The tracks that *langlaufers* use were for years stamped out by volunteers, but at the 1960 Winter Olympics in Squaw Valley track-making machines were used for the first time. Snow-making equipment now helps as well. By compacting the powder snow and carving a furrow through even the hardest surfaces, track-making machines have revolutionised the sport and at the same time made it possible to put in more than one lane. Cries of 'Track!', by those hemmed in behind, are now heard less frequently and, because the piste is rolled, those who 'skate' do less damage to the tracks than previously.

Pistes packed down for 'skaters' tend to keep in better shape than tracks cut for classical skiers which may quickly get iced up and full of ruts. It is also easier to learn to 'skate' using the edges of the skis rather than to perfect the more difficult classical method of preventing the skis sliding backwards. Classical skiers also need to know about the intricacies of waxing, which are not so important to the 'skater'. Many classical races have been won by wax alone and the Italians, with their secret Cera wax, have held a technological advantage for several years that, some would argue, has little to do with skiing.

Opposite: One disadvantage of the skating style is that skiers are not always able to pass each other, often resulting in some interesting international language.

HIGH WAY OVER THE ALPS

There is another way of skiing cross-country, known as ski touring. One famous tour through the French and Swiss Alps is called the High Route, which the author described in 'High Way Over the Alps', *The Field*, June 1963.

The High Route or Haute-Route crosses the tallest mountain country in Europe; more than 50 miles of skiing across the roof of the world, an escape to fresh sparkling air and wide blue horizons. Here from Chamonix in the French Alps to Zermatt and Saas Fee in the Swiss Alps, the glaciers are the path and the great peaks the signposts. Only the snow conditions, the position of the refuge huts and the state of wind and limb seem to dictate the route.

But part of our particular route depended on one other factor, that the guide we had hired from Verbier had to be in church at Zermatt on Sunday. By then it was Wednesday, so armed with skins (bands of mock sealskin attached to downhill skis to prevent them from sliding backwards) and climbing tackle, peanuts and pumpernickel, we set out in a hurry for the Cabin Mont Fort [now accessible by cable car!] high above Verbier. It was to be a five-day nightmare that none of our party of five men and two girls, all proficient skiers, would wish to repeat. . . . At Easter in the High Alps it is necessary to start out from the refuge huts at first light and to finish your march by midday, for it is much easier to

climb and descend when the snow is hard, and before it becomes dangerous in the afternoon sunshine. On that day we tried too hard and, rounding a shoulder in mid afternoon, there was a dreadful earsplitting crash as half the mountain broke away in front of us, engulfing a party of Frenchmen, the only other people we were to see during the entire expedition.

Later, as we made our way towards the summit of the Pigne d'Arolla, it became apparent that we were hopelessly lost. At first there had been a few flurries of snow, but then, as the wind increased to a frenzy and drove icy particles into face and clothing, the rope became a precious lifeline. We dug a snow hole, and as the cloud momentarily lifted, we could see underneath us a terrifying ice wall curving away into the mist, whilst on either side massive rock buttresses could be followed some 2,000ft into the dreadful abyss below. I had somehow managed to squeeze toothpaste on my face instead of suncream and everyone thought I was about to pass out.

Our bedraggled arrival in Zermatt could hardly have been described as heroic, indeed so badly were we afflicted by snow blindness that our welcoming loved ones could only be identified by feel! Not all touring on skis need be so exacting, indeed it can be one of the more peaceful yet exhilarating experiences in life.

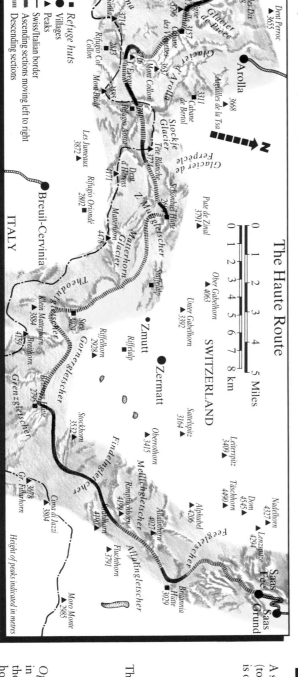

48

The Haute Route

Refuge huts
Peaks
Villages
Swiss/Italian border
Ascending sections moving left to right
Descending sections

Height of peaks indicated in metres

Dent Perroc 3655
Cabane des Dix 2928
Mont Blanc de Cheilon 3870
Glacier de Cheilon
Glacier de Tsena
La Serpentine 3579
Pigne d'Arolla 3796
Glacier d'Otemma
La Sengla
3713
Arolla
Mont Collon 3637
3831
Aiguilles de la Tsa 3668
Serpentine
Ruinette
Col Collon 3875
Stockje Glacier
Tête Blanche 3724
Dents d'Hérens 4171
Rifugio Col Collon
Les Jumeaux 3872
Rifugio Oriondé 2802
Breuil-Cervinia
Stockje Glacier
Zmuttgletscher
Schönbiel Hütte
Pointe de Zinal 3791
Ober Gabelhorn 4063
Unter Gabelhorn 3392
Zmutt
Riffelalp
Riffelhorn 2928
Schwartzee
Stellisee
Klein Matterhorn 3884
Matterhorn 4478
Breithorn 4159
Theodulgletscher
Gornergletscher
Zermatt
Sattelspitz 3164
Oberrothorn 3415
Stockhorn 3532
Findelngletscher
Cima di Jazzi 3804
Mono Monte 2985
Gr. Fillarhorn
Leiterspitz 3409
Täschhorn 4490
Dom 4545
Nadelhorn 4327
Lenzspitze 4294
Alphubel 4206
Rimpfischhorn 4199
Allalinhorn 4027
Feegletscher
Britannia Hütte 3029
Allalingletscher
Fluchthorn 3791
3678
Saas Fee
Saas Grund

N

ITALY
SWITZERLAND

0 1 2 3 4 5 6 7 8 km
0 1 2 3 4 5 Miles

The Haute Route
Breney and Otemma Glaciers

A section of the High Route looking towards the Matterhorn (top centre) and Zermatt in the valley beyond. The precise route is optional.

The High Route from Verbier to Saas Fee.

Opposite: The High Route crosses the tallest mountain country in Europe; more than 50 miles (80km) of skiing across the roof of the world, an escape to clear sparkling air and wide blue horizons.

Track

HELP!

The story of the High Route would not be complete if it did not include a helicopter rescue. The Frenchmen mentioned in the last section were indeed dug out by our party although two were badly injured by falling rocks and one, the last we located, was crushed and very close to death. Fortunately we found that a tunnel was being dug through the mountains close by, and having climbed down a ventilator shaft we were able, eventually by telephone, to summon the famous Alpine pilot Hermann Geiger, to the scene. He flew out the injured immediately and through his prompt action two of the three men were saved.

For those who prefer to dice with death on the two- or four-man bob (depicted here in about 1910), there are no worries about mountain rescue services. Bobs, although sturdily built, are prone to mechanical failure. It has been known for a runner to fall off, or for the steering to jam, hurling the bob out of control into the trees, as happened on one tragic occasion at St Moritz with fatal consequences to the entire four-man crew. Any misjudgement by the driver, such as getting into a corner too late and too high, is likely to result in a heavy fall, and should the brakeman be knocked out of his seat, which is not uncommon, the result is usually most satisfactory for the accident clinics. Bobbers therefore throw themselves down the run with the knowledge that at least one patient 'vulture' with his 'blood wagon' is waiting for them beside the track.

Rescue in the mountains, much like rescue at sea, is sometimes a matter of luck. But the odds of disaster may now be greatly reduced if a radio is carried when climbing or skiing off-piste, and if the party all wear avalanche bleepers. So often a party set out in brilliant weather, whatever the time of year, only to see the storm clouds roll in and the 'picnic' suddenly turn to panic. Many disasters are caused by a senseless lack of responsibility: no training, no proper equipment, no understanding of weather and snow conditions, no knowledge or indication of the route, and very often no use of a professional guide. Any one of these omissions may kill, and it very often does.

Mountain Rescue services, similarly to the lifeboat service, are usually manned by local volunteers. There is little standard training, but all must be competent skiers or climbers with a knowledge of snowcraft. First aid, avalanche drill and transportation of the injured, is normally taught on locally run courses. North America and Japan, however, have their own specialist centrally organised and have their own specialist Mountain Rescue career structures.

Most ski resorts now employ a professional rescue manager and a number of senior patrolmen nominated as team leaders should there be a disaster. Some accident clinics organise their own rescue teams. Where helicopters are used for ski transport they are normally available for rescue work, and over half the casualties in the mountains are now assisted from the air.

Hermann Geiger was one of the earliest pilots to develop the use of aircraft for Alpine rescue and the first to make regular landings on Alpine snowfields and glaciers. Starting by carrying provisions and equipment into remote mountain areas, he perfected the technique of touching down on steep slopes and slewing to a stop on the tiniest pinnacles. It was a hazardous business at the best of times, but as he became increasingly involved in rescue work, the weather, which was usually appalling, made his task even more difficult. His first diminutive Piper Cub had only basic instruments and no de-icing mechanism, and often, not knowing what jagged peak lay below, he would have to spiral down through holes in the shifting clouds to prevent the wings freezing over. On one occasion, as he was about to land, he was thrown 150ft (45m) into the air by the blast from a mighty avalanche.

On a clear sunlit day during the summer of 1966, Geiger was making his final approach at a small airfield nestling in a valley of his native Swiss Alps when he collided with a glider and died instantly as his aircraft plunged into the ground. It seemed rough justice for a man who was always 'nose down and tail up' and the much respected pioneer of the *Rettungsflugwacht*, air rescue in the high mountains.

Helicopters have two main disadvantages as air rescue vehicles: they are unable to land on sloping ground and are expensive to operate.

Left: A ski-mountaineering victim is hoisted clear from a rocky platform, having been carried there as a less likely area to be hit by avalanches.

Preparing for the run down (*oil pinting by Gemalde von O. Ackermann-Pasegg, 1932*)

SKI
MOUNTAINEERING

Mountaineering on skis in general terms begins when the skier, armed with rope and ice-axe, crosses the summer snowline. It ends when, usually after a desperate fight against the elements, the skier eventually returns home safely in one piece, having negotiated the unknown precipices and icefalls.

At first, even amongst the early converts to the joys of skiing, there was a certain prejudice against ski mountaineering, and a Swiss pioneer wrote: 'Skis were left behind on winter climbs . . . For a long time we could not eliminate our strong aversion to the uncertainty of movement on ski and from the imprisonment of one's feet in the bindings.'

Ski mountaineering really started in 1896 when Wilhelm Paulcke, probably one of the earliest Germans on skis, with a small party scaled the Oberalpstock in the first ski ascent of any mountain exceeding 10,000ft (3,000m). In the following year he underlined this feat by traversing on skis the length of the Bernese Oberland.

In 1898, for a ski attempt on Monte Rosa, the highest mountain in Switzerland, Paulcke chose as his companion the well-known climber Dr Robert Helbling, a man who had until then 'looked upon this method of progression with sovereign contempt'! Although the attempt failed, Helbling must have been impressed, for he wrote later: 'Paulcke prend les devants, filant comme une fleche, le corps incline en avant, fouillant l'avant-terrain du regard afin d'eviter les crevasses, de trouver le bon chemin, et de s'y maintenir' (Paulcke covered the ground travelling as straight as an arrow, his body leaning forward, scanning the way ahead for crevasses, in order to find the best route and keep his balance). A few weeks later Monte Rosa was scaled on ski by the German mountaineer Oscar Schuster; since then many famous men have tackled its difficult slopes, including Sir Winston Churchill, who later became Prime Minister of England.

Wilhelm Paulcke.

Opposite: Skis often have to be abandoned on the final rock or ice ridges of a peak.

Some para-skiers are not so lucky. This novice unfortunately drifted into a ski-lift and was wound painfully into the mechanism. It took some time to release the badly injured man and his parachute.

SKI GLIDING

Para-gliding and hang-gliding with skis are probably the two best ways of getting down a mountain quickly without knowing more than how to point your feet in the right direction. Many visit the mountains in winter for reasons other than skiing, some to try their hand at curling, perhaps or tobogganing; others to race their cars on ice (until the authorities stopped the sport in Switzerland, arguing that the fumes were killing the fish!). Perhaps ski-gliding kills off the birds, as it may have done once — with laughter!

The first 'ski pilot' to combine hang-gliding with ski-ing was probably Jeff Jobe from Washington DC in 1970. Before then it was necessary to run like hell in order to get airborne, or alternatively to throw oneself over a cliff. Jobe saw it differently, and by skiing

steeply downhill into the wind, he developed the per-fect means of take-off. The perfect landing, fortu-nately, followed. Jobe, who later went on a barnstorm-ing tour of most major skiing resorts in the United States, lifting off every decent peak he could find, quickly fired the imagination of others and soon many skiers were learning to fly, and flyers to ski. Within a few years ski-gliding had become a major attraction at most resorts around the world. Ski-gliding schools were established in many places, and for a few 'bucks' it became possible to take an exhilarating flight as a passenger.

Para-skiing, or parachuting with skis, started much earlier. By stretching out the arms whilst 'schussing' downhill, skiers had discovered that the air-brake effect was impressive. Add Superman's bat's wings and you were up, up, and away — or so they thought! The advent of the multi-directional sport parachute, how-ever, has now made life in the 'fast lane' much easier.

Hang-glider.

Up, up, and away. Para-skiing 1938 style.

Opposite: Para-skiing in the French Alps. The advent of the multi-directional sport parachute has now made life much easier. Parachutes have also been developed to pull skiers up the mountain in the right breeze.

SKIKJÖRING

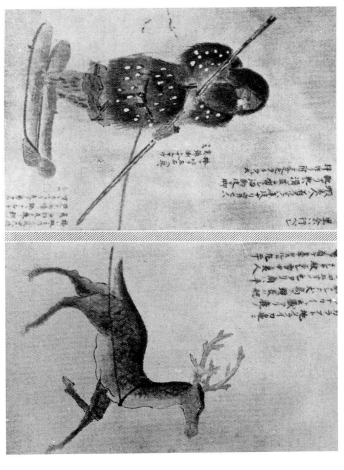

The 'white turf', as it is romantically called, is usually prepared on the Alpine lakes towards the end of January. By then the ice can be as thick as 20in (50cm) and should have a good covering of snow. Bulldozers or Snowcats are used to prepare a 160ft (50m) wide piste and, as if to titillate the appetite for the sport which is to follow, it is not uncommon for a machine to fall through the ice and cause a considerable sensation.

Skikjöring or snörekjöring as it was originally called (though there is nothing sleepy about the sport!) was dreamed up by the Lapps who, by harnessing their reindeer, had found them as useful as Father Christmas did for pulling their heavy sledges. No doubt, as time passed, they were soon racing each other for the odd pile of birch logs, and from that probably developed the idea of being dragged behind on skis.

Skikjöring was introduced to Central Europe by an enthusiast, Mr Saratz from Pontresina in Switzerland, at about the turn of the century. He had managed to acquire some reindeer from Norway and started off by holding several demonstrations. The first race, skied more sensibly behind horses, was staged on a road, the ice on the lake being unsafe, at St Moritz, Switzerland, in March 1906. It was won by Billy Griggs, who was later to be the mentor of the famous British jockey and trainer Sir Gordon Richards.

Today skikjöring continues as a magnificent spectacle, combined now with trotting races started a few years later; flat racing, introduced from 1911; hurdling which was included in about 1920; and recently polo which is equally exciting played on ice. Skikjöring requires considerable skill, particularly in restraining the animal (horses gallop faster on snow), and skikjörers often finish in considerable disarray – sometimes, as happened in St Moritz in 1965, with not a single 'jockey' reaching the winning post.

Although officially the sport of skiing was not introduced into Japan until 1902, Professor W. Knoll from Hamburg, West Germany, wrote an article in the 1930 edition of *Der Winter* which stated that the Japanese were using skis long before then. This is as mentioned in a book published in 1804, *Eine Reife nach dem Morden Japans*. Perhaps the earliest use of skis in Japan was snörekjöring behind reindeer as depicted in this ancient ink drawing.

Right: Before the age of the motor vehicle it was not uncommon for whole families to go skikjöring on a winter's afternoon.

Left: On the snow-covered tundra of northern Norway, better known as Lapland.

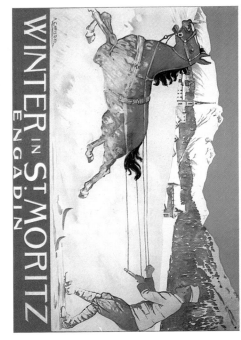

Skikjöring requires considerable skill, particularly in restraining the animal. In ski centres other than St Moritz, the horses are now usually ridden.

Opposite: Snörekjöring, as practised by the Lapps.

ICED WATER

In *Skiing the Skyline* Arnold Lunn wrote:

Glacier skiing in spring has a charm of its own, particularly where the slope is steep enough for speed but not steep enough for a turn. On the smooth unchanging gradients of a gentle glacier you lose the sense of personal movement. You feel as if you were stationary and as if it were your surroundings that are moving. Your skis seem like a narrow skiff anchored in midstream, a slender boat that sways gently as the river sweeps round the bows. The illusion is reinforced when you reach the wrinkled limits of the snows. As your speed relaxes the foreground that had rushed up to meet you slows down and the magic network of dancing shadow and fugitive light sobers into successive ridges of cracked and gleaming ice. Suddenly the world gives a little jerk. The mountains stop moving and the world of fancy gives way to the world of fact.

Arnold Lunn's enduring love of the mountains probably came more from ski mountaineering than from downhill skiing. He continues:

Winter is never so visibly Queen of the High Alps as in the month that sees her passing, for the damp clinging snow of late spring finds a resting place on rocks and ice from which the dry powder snow of winter is torn off by the first gust of wind.

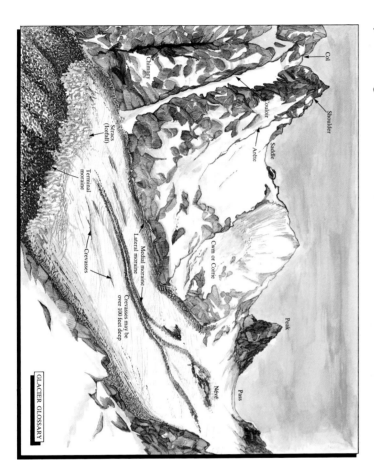

At this time of year, the best for glacier skiing, slopes of bare scree often mingle with those which are gleaming white where there has been a sudden snow shower or perhaps snow has remained on a face shaded from the heat of the sun. The effect is dramatic.

A few years ago one of the most exciting expeditions in spring was to ski the Eismeer Glacier above Kleine Scheidegg in the Swiss Alps. Taking the railway which winds through a tunnel towards the summit of the Jungfrau, and getting out at one point to look down the sheer wall of the dreaded north face of the Eiger, it was possible at the next station to cut a doorway with an ice-axe through the snow from comparative darkness into the glare of this lovely glacier. But sadly the once well-skied Eismeer, which winds its way down behind a massive range of mountains to Grindelwald, has been receding so fast that it is no longer possible to exit over the icefalls that block the neck of the valley below. Not so all glaciers; many are growing, and some have a nasty habit of spitting out, possibly more than half a century later, the well-preserved bodies of those who once fell into their yawning crevasses.

Sometimes it is hot work picking your way down through the crevasses exposed after a long winter by the spring sunshine. There is no shortage of iced water at the glacier's exit, but look out for bodies!

Chamois are spotted frequently when spring skiing in the Alps.

Lugging skis along rocky paths on the Grossglockner, Austria, 1930s.

SPRING FEVER

For those who have not experienced the exhilaration of skiing the glaciers, there is one other treat that the mountains have in store towards the end of the season; it is known, sometimes worshipped, as 'spring snow'.

Following days of hot spring sunshine the snow becomes soft during the day but overnight it freezes, thus creating a hard surface over the entire mountainside. At first the snow is iced with crystals which shine like satin in the morning sunlight, but as the surface begins to warm up, it develops a thin layer of gossamer that makes turning on skis as easy as slicing a knife through butter. Skiers, having once sampled its subtle delights, will search for spring-snow like pirates after chests of gold. Spring snow hunting quickly becomes a fever: 'Where? What height? At what time?' are the urgent questions asked in the 'stubli' before turning in at night, and in the morning careful note is taken of the maximum-minimum thermometer and of the day's weather, which is most likely to be glorious. Before setting out it is necessary to plan the route carefully and, if possible, to choose a place for a late lunch with a shaded piste which still has snow on it. The art is to start with the sun and end with the sun, never allowing it to linger too long on any one slope before you reach it. It is therefore necessary to start skiing at breakfast on the eastern slopes and then move to the western slopes by early afternoon. Knowledge of the local terrain is essential for, unlike skiing in powder snow earlier in the season, a mistaken route may often result in hours of wasted time, lugging skis over grassy meadows or along endless stretches of rocky mountainside.

Spring-snow skiing is a sensation that once tried is never forgotten. The skis hiss through the snow without the least resistance and it is possible to carve swooping 'aeroplane' turns over the folds in the mountain with effortless 'skill' and 'professionalism'. Only a tree root may be likely to interrupt, and spoil the majesty of the occasion.

In spring it is fun to carve swooping 'aeroplane' turns over the folds in the mountain.

Opposite: Spring skiing near Nuria in the Spanish Pyrenees.

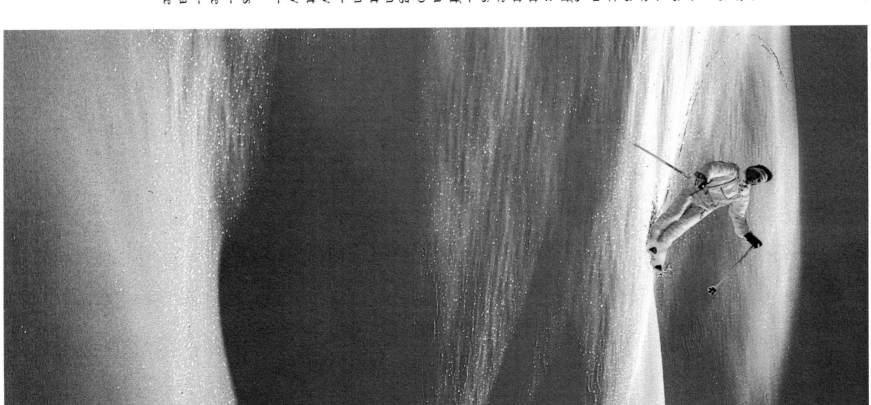

SKING THE YEAR ROUND

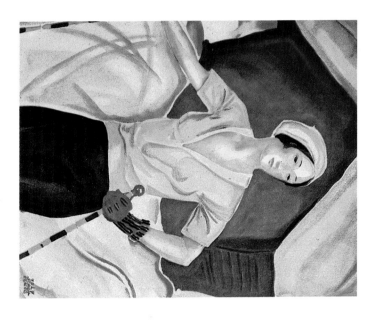

Serious ski-racers chase the winter round the globe, skiing from November until April or May in the Alps before moving to the southern hemisphere, to New Zealand and Australia, to Portillo in Chile or further south to Bariloche in the Argentine. With them will go a crowd of ski instructors, for just as New Zealand sheep shearers may cross the world during the summer in search of work, many ski instructors travel equally widely to earn themselves a living through the cold months of winter. But such skiers are more the exception than the rule. 'What has been your longest season?', the author once asked his guide. 'Five years' came the surprising reply. Summer skiing, however, is different.

In many of the great skiing areas of the world where the snow lies in summer above 8,500ft (2,600m), it is now possible to ski the whole year round. Of course it has always been possible, if the skier was prepared to climb. Recently the helicopter and high altitude ski-lift have added a whole new dimension to skiing under the summer sun. Apart from climbing as an art itself, there is little to match the experience of shouldering skis across green meadows dashed with the colour of bright mountain flowers, and then ascending by the most convenient means to a tiny patch of ice glinting on some distant pinnacle. In Kashmir, where many of the

people are desperately poor, summer visitors with skis are sometimes carried up the foothills of the Himalyas by porters in search of snow. Perhaps, if the porters had any sense, they would drop them down the most convenient precipice on the other side!

Summer skiers do not always burn black all over; bikini skiing is the exception rather than the rule. At high altitude, skiing short runs down the smooth névés of the glaciers is not as blisteringly hot as some may think, indeed it can be freezing—cold enough for snow to lie there all the year round. Only around mid morning does the surface slowly begin to thaw, when for about an hour conditions are blissful, the sun is glorious, and the views of the peaks magnificent, stretching like a white canopy far away over the dark valleys below. Later, when the snow has melted to porridge, there is every excuse to descend by lift for lunch and to spend the rest of the day 'free', playing tennis or basking by a swimming pool until the tanning job is done.

Opposite: Summer skiing in the Italian Dolomites. Some ski resorts are close enough to the sea for a little after-lunch water-skiing.

Summer skiing has always been possible, if the skier was prepared to climb (*oil painting by Alfons Walde, 1928*).

Today some thirty Alpine ski resorts offer summer skiing. In America several ski areas stay open during the summer, such as Timberline in Oregon, which has lifts up to 8,500ft (2,600m), and sits almost on top of a volcano, Mount Hood.

INFERNO

Competitor in the Inferno, 1931.

One of the most famous racers to win the trophy on the Inferno course was the British girl Esme 'Muffie' Mackinnon, winner of both the Ladies World Downhill and Slalom Championships in 1931. Approaching the finish at Lauterbrunnen, she was confronted by a funeral procession and stopped to pay her respects. Count Bonacossa, an admiring Italian official, kindly adjusted her time.

James Bond liked his vodka Martinis shaken and not stirred. When, in 1969, *On Her Majesty's Secret Service* was filmed at Mürren, the venue in 1931 of the first World Downhill and Slalom Championships and the home of the dreaded Inferno, the delights of summer skiing were far from the director's mind. What he wanted was macho, hard gritted stuff – Mürren madness.

Mürren, its name derived from *murus*, Latin for 'wall', breathes macho, for it sits perched precariously on a 2,600ft (800m) precipice above the valley of Lauterbrunnen in the Swiss Alps. The first hotel was opened there in 1857 and, largely due to the efforts of the master travel agent Henry Lunn, Sir Arnold's father, it was one of the earliest ski resorts in Central Europe, and the first place in Switzerland to erect a ski tow. Now, mercifully for most racers, the cablecar that connects the village to the summit of the Schilthorn, 9,745ft (2,970m), built with financial aid from Mr Bond, saves skiers the 5½ hour climb on skis that, from the Inferno's inception in 1928, used to be all part of the course.

The Inferno, which once had a *geschmozzle* (mass) start, is a race without gates except where you dive into the 'Gun Barrel' in a mad plunge for the valley 7,500ft (2,300m) below. It is a January free-for-all, an opportunity for amateurs to pit themselves against often intolerable off-piste snow conditions in the very worst kind of weather. Popularised as an international event by Toni Heibeler, the first man to conquer the north face of the Eiger in winter, it is not for the faint hearted. In 1954 Field Marshal Viscount Montgomery of Alamein, then President of the Kandahar Club, began advertising the race to teams from the NATO armed forces, and since then it has never looked back. Today as many as 1,400 skiers, the maximum permitted, still compete for trophies in the Inferno. Since its foundation by the Kandahar Club the course, which has some uphill sections and is never groomed, has always tested a racer's skills and powers of endurance to the limit, and at 8¾ miles (14km) it has remained the longest Downhill race in the world.

Dead Man's Gulch, Glencoe. Scottish Kandahar, 1956.

In 1907 the National Ski Club for Scotland was formed with Dr William Bruce in the chair. Dr Bruce, who ran the high-altitude observatory on Ben Nevis, had obtained his skis from the famous Arctic explorer Fridtjof Nansen. Since then the facilities have been steadily improved and Scotland has become a popular skiing area for those who enjoy the bagpipes and are suitably hardy. Conditions at Scottish ski resorts – such as Aviemore in the beautiful Cairngorms, or Glencoe, where the Campbells once massacred the sleeping Macdonalds – may be idyllic in spring but sometimes, as blizzards howl across the hills and racers thread their way through rock-strewn corries, they seem to have something in common with the rigours of their Swiss counterpart, the Inferno.

Opposite: Competitors in the Inferno often pit themselves against intolerable conditions. To the left background is the windswept north face of the Eiger, to the right the forbidding crags of the Black Monk, a hunting ground for eagles.

SKI SOLDIERS

An early form of biathlon – but for real. Norway 1808.

White ski clothing often distinguishes mountain troops – if they can be spotted against the snow.

Members of Captain Scott's ill fated expedition to the South Pole in 1913 had been taught to ski, or so Scott believed, by Lieutenant Tryggve Gran, an Officer in the Norwegian army. Scott had written in his diary: 'December 16th. It is very difficult to know what to do about ski. Their weight is considerable and yet under certain circumstances, they are extraordinarily useful'. And then on 18 December: 'Left skis behind and started marching without them . . . skis are the thing and here are my tiresome fellow countrymen too predjudiced to have prepared themselves for the event.' Such an error of judgement, which probably influenced the course of the disaster, must have been a salutary lesson to any military skier who later read about the deaths of the gallant Captain Scott and his misguided comrades.

Apart from the use of skis for hunting, their purpose before skiing became a sport in the nineteenth century, was primarily military. Skis were the ideal way of moving fast across snow-covered ground in winter, and as far back as the twelfth century it was recorded that the Finns waged war on skis. In 1806 it was noted that Swedish ski soldiers were armed with a bayonet-type ski-stick and later the distinctive white clothing worn by ski troops became a familiar sight in the mountains of many northern countries. By the early 1900s military ski units had been formed not only throughout Scandinavia but also in Russia, Austria and Germany, based on long distance cross-country disciplines. In the United States, Canada, France, Switzerland, Spain and Italy, however, greater attention was paid to downhill running. World War II saw ski troops in action on a grand scale in Europe, and the US 10th Mountain Division, the French Chasseurs Alpins, and the Italian Alpini were amongst those, including many gallant British and Scandinavians, who particularly distinguished themselves.

The Swiss, however, because the country is prepared to defend its neutrality in any possible situation, now have one of the best organised ski militia of any army in the world. Conscripted to learn about mountain warfare soon after leaving school, most Swiss males are attached to the army until they reach the age of 54. Meanwhile each household has to stock a permanent supply of emergency rations plus arms and ammunition, and all new houses have to be built with nuclear shelters, or 'ski-rooms' as they are more likely to be named.

At the 1948 St Moritz Olympics cross-country skiing was included, instead of running, in the modern pentathlon, itself the brainchild of de Coubertin, architect of the Olympic Games as we know them today. But, because horses were not always easy to come by in the mountains for the riding event, this form of pentathlon was never repeated. The biathlon, a derivative of the pentathlon and an ideal competition for ski troops, was not, however, included in the Olympics until 1960 at Squaw Valley. In the biathlon each competitor, whilst racing over a 12½ mile (20km) cross-country course, has to stop four times to fire a rifle, which must be carried between stages on the back. It is not easy to shoot from a standing position, particularly when desperately short of breath, but, cruelly, a 2-minute penalty is added for each missed target.

Opposite: Ski patrol in Norway.

'Ja, im Felde, da zeighten wir jederzeit als Skikameraden Gebirglerschneid' ('Yes, we are always great comrades in mountain warfare') (painted by R. Mahn)

HITTING THE EASTERN TRAILS

Skiing in the United States of America is often a flattering experience. Snow conditions always seem to be a little more predictable, soft snow a little softer and the piste a little smoother than in Europe. Some call it the 'American dream'.

The main ski areas in America are situated either on the East Coast or in the West and they vie with each other for top honours. Easterners say that only their snow is always predictably good, largely due to their sophisticated snow-making and grooming equipment, while Westerners say that their powder snow is the best in the world. Both claims, from regions which are entirely different in character, are probably correct.

Trail skiing is the name of the game on the East Coast where there are now a surprisingly wide choice of skiing areas. But although the sport, influenced by Norwegians, had started in New Hampshire with the formation of the Nansen Club, Berlin, at the turn of the century, it has undergone a long period of gestation. A number of trails were cleared there during the thirties, and in 1932 Woodstock, Vermont, installed America's very first drag lift. But it was not until after World War II, when the US Forest Service assumed a prominent role in ski-area development, that skiing really took off. As a result many of the hills on the East Coast, owned largely by the US government, now look in summer like the shaven heads of an African tribe or alternatively a vast golf course, its fairways swathed through endless forests of birch and maple. Here in winter, instead of golf trolleys, squadrons of snowcats can be seen grooming the gleaming white trails, and long after sundown their lights are visible far up in the mountains – busy like a swarm of fire-flies.

Many of these eastern ski areas, often started in collaboration with mountain guides from Europe, lie within easy reach of New York or other American cities, and in order to cope with weekend traffic their administration has to be outstanding. Swift multiplace chairlifts make queuing a problem of the past, well-staffed ski schools cope with every appetite, fast food restaurants top up energy levels over the briefest 'pit stop', and a multitude of well-prepared pistes, spread overnight with a liberal coating of man-made snow, make skiing almost effortless.

Insurance in America is outrageously expensive and every attempt is made to reduce risk on the pistes. Modern snow-making equipment consisting of compressed air and water guns consuming up to 800gal (3,638 litres) per minute, if used often at night even when it is snowing 'naturally', may keep pistes in perfect condition over an extended skiing season. Man-made snow, laced with special additives, can now be laid at temperatures over 2 degrees above freezing and its gritty texture prevents it evaporating as quickly as the snow from heaven. But snow making is expensive, costing Stratton Mountain, for example, over $1,500,000 per year. Fortunately for US ski resorts, American skiers will drive much further to the snowfields than their European counterparts – particularly if they know that good skiing conditions can be guaranteed.

Snow-making equipment is now so effective that all 250 acres (100 ha) of Hunter Mountain, a ski centre just outside New York city, can be covered with 5ft (1.5m) of man-made snow (it is not 'artificial') over a single night.

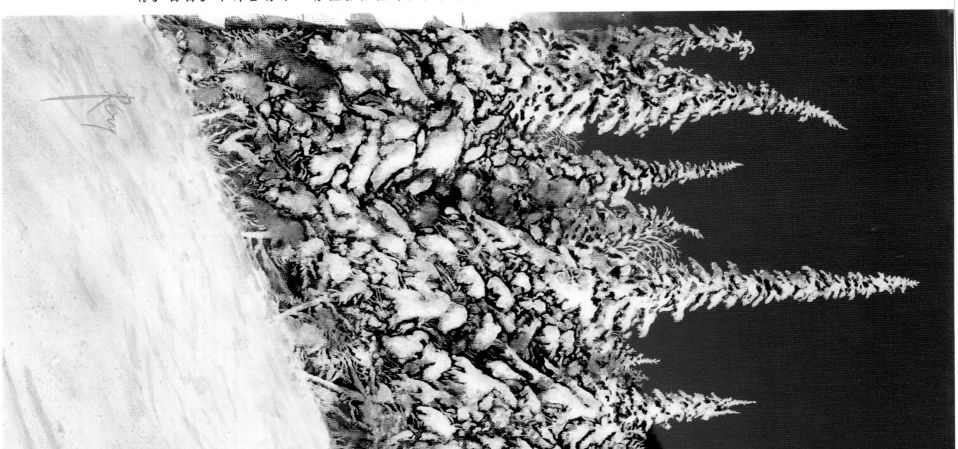

Opposite: Most ski trails in America are immaculately groomed.

Emo Henrich, head of the ski school, has been at Stratton Mountain since it was first developed for skiing in 1960, soon after he had left his native Austria. A talented artist and musician, his Tyrolean charm is quickly forgotten when confronting reckless skiers.

Stratton Mountain, at 3,936ft (1,200m) is one of the highest peaks in Vermont. I first skied at Stratton during March. There was a frightful smell before I entered the village and I thought it was the drains. 'Never', replied my indignant host, 'it is the first smell of spring – an awakening skunk!' (Watercolour by Linda Roberts.)

POWDER IN THE WILD WEST

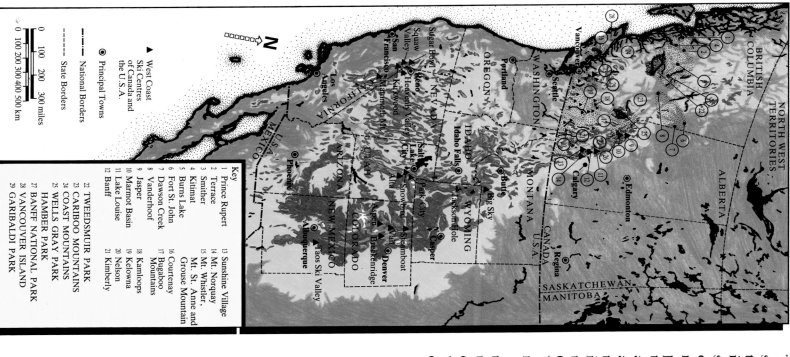

The magnificent range of the Rocky Mountains which stretch from Canada southwards over almost the entire length of the United States, and the Sierra Nevada in California, now provide a winter playground for skiers which is hard to beat. One of the earliest records of skiing in the Rockies is of John L. Dyer, a Methodist minister who in the 1850s used skis to visit his parishioners in Colorado. But although it is known that Norwegian miners organised a few competitions amongst themselves at places like Crested Butte soon after this, the sport, which had started with the formation of America's first ski club at La Porte, California, in 1867, for a long time lagged behind developments in the east. Only in 1935, when the first National Ski Championships were held at Paradise Valley and the Westerners missed out, was action taken to make the region more accessible.

Today not only have roads been driven into most of the best areas, but several new ski resorts have sprung up from nowhere—such as Vail in Colorado, the brainchild of a war hero from the 10th Mountain Division, who built it in just one year, 1962, at an estimated cost of $5,000,000. Skiers will now travel any distance to

Vail or to Aspen, skiing's Hollywood, named after its beautiful trees, where in 1890 Colorado miners unearthed the largest silver nugget (weighing more than a ton) ever found. Park City and Snowbird in Utah, Jackson Hole in Wyoming, Heavenly Valley and Squaw Valley in California and many other Western resorts including those in Montana and Washington, have become equally well known.

Much of the best skiing in the Rockies is high above the timberline, but where there are trees there are also extensive trails. Rocky Mountain powder, if you can get there before the rest of mankind, has a quality which surprises even the true virgin-snow connoisseur. The atmosphere is so dry in the Rockies and the winter temperature so cold that the snow, composed of larger more diffused crystals than elsewhere, is so light that it may billow above the skiers' heads as they glide gloriously downhill with the surface well over their knees. It is the most exciting powder skiing to be found almost anywhere in the world.

Opposite: The Rockies provide a perfect winter playground. In the Wild West they keep their powder dry!

HELISKING

One way to get at powder snow before anyone else can spoil it with their signature, is to fly out to your favourite peak by helicopter. It sounds easy, but very often it is not.

During the fifties and early sixties, when Hermann Geiger and his friends were skilfully landing their fixed-wing aircraft high up on the glaciers, all was well, but with the advent of the noisier gas-turbine high performance helicopter, the environmentalists started to object. Worse still, there were many ardent climbers who complained very strongly when, after an exhausting slog up the mountain, they were beaten to it by a crowd of unfit tycoons who had tumbled out of a helicopter. So heated were the accusations that glacier flights in the Alps were forbidden and other landing areas confined to just a few designated zones. Not so in the Canadian Rockies, though, and all at once there started the new, if somewhat exclusive, sport of organised heliskiing.

Ardent powder hounds had long set their sights on the untrammelled snowfields of the Canadian Rockies, but communications were almost non existent and cross-country access virtually impossible. However, in 1966, an Austrian immigrant, Hans Gmoser, began organising helicopter flights from Banff into the Monashees, the Cariboos and then the Bugaboos, a vast area of magnificent skiing country on the British Colombian side of the Rockies, where it was unnecessary to ski the same slope, let alone the same mountain, twice in the same season!

Everything in Canada has to be on a vast scale, and even the helicopters carry at least a dozen passengers – far more than in the Alps. But the lodges in these remote mountains have no access roads so everything, even the bread and clean linen, has to be flown in by air. Flying over the dense pine forests of the foothills, one soon gets an impression of the immensity of it all; but nothing puts skiers more on their metal than talk of 'tree holes' (cavities left under the fir branches into which is it possible to disappear completely) and 'ski tracers' (ribbons of fluorescent orange material which, when skis are released in a fall, mark them, thankfully, in the bottomless powder).

Everything has to be flown in by helicopter, including the skiers.

Skiers in Canada must beware of bears! The earliest record of skiing in Canada is of a Norwegian labourer in 1857, although a hundred years earlier a pair of skis from Greenland had apparently been displayed at a Canadian ice carnival. Canadian skiers have since become among the best in the world. Apart from the Rockies, Canada can also provide good skiing in the Laurentian Mountains to the east.

First run of the morning far north in the Bugaboos. The helicopter will follow the skiers down then pluck them away to other virgin snowfields.

72

SKI EXTREME

There are several ways to die skiing; it is a dangerous sport, but the surest way is to try skiing several thousand feet down a 50 to 60 degree snow precipice. That is precisely what Sylvain Saudan set out to achieve when in October 1969 he launched himself off the top of the Aiguille de Bionnassay, a 13,000ft (4,000m) peak in France which is the steepest and iciest slope on which such a descent was then, and still is, considered possible. Amazingly he survived.

Saudan, a Swiss mountain guide considered by many to be crazy, is only one of a growing number of skiers (among them the ex-President of France, Giscard d'Estaing, credited many years ago with the second descent of the north face of Mount Blanc) who have taken downhill skiing to the limit. Amongst others Heini Holzer from Italy and Gerhard Winter, one of the early pioneers from Austria, are particularly well known for their daring. Foolhardiness, no; the planning is meticulous. Holzer tackles the problem differently from Saudan, for whereas Saudan usually makes a detailed reconnaissance of each awesome slope by helicopter, Holzer climbs them, if they are climbable, in order to choose his precise route down from the ground. Safety equipment is hardly considered, sharp edges to skis and points to the sticks are essential, but the rest is a gamble with death. Although both skiers will then descend in a rapid, almost staccato, succession of turns, Holzer jumps but Saudan just bounces. There is one other ski maniac, however, Yuichiro Miura, who prefers to take it straight!

Miura, one of Japan's great post-war heroes, in May 1970 attempted the incredible feat of skiing from above the dizzy heights of the South Col of Mount Everest down a sheer slope to the Western Cwm, a terrifying drop of over 4,000ft (1,300m). Near the base of this icy wall, which is so steep that it has never been climbed, a bottomless crevasse awaited its first victim. Miura relied entirely on a parachute to break his speed, which he calculated would open in the rarefied atmosphere at about 108mph (175kph). It opened, but failed to slow him down. He fell and slid to a halt within a few hair-raising feet of the crevasse.

Cresta Run, St Moritz, Switzerland, c1900. Approaching Shuttlecock corner.

Sitting in the old Victorian hut at Top with spiked boots propped against a red-hot stove, the Cresta rider could be accused of enjoying himself – if it were not that his stomach, already denied breakfast, was secretly gripped by fear. Pushing off down a corridor of ice, on the sound of a bell, might be called fun if there were not a violent succession of death-defying corners waiting menacingly below. Screaming round the lip of Shuttlecock with only an inch of ice to spare, could be described as the second greatest sensation on earth – but only if the rider avoids being catapulted with his lead-heavy toboggan, hard into the beckoning hay. So what is so special about the Cresta Run, the 'grownup's garden slide'? Nothing different from a skier dropping off the top of a near vertical mountain, perhaps?

(Beginners – the Cresta is solo only – start lower down the run from Junction.)

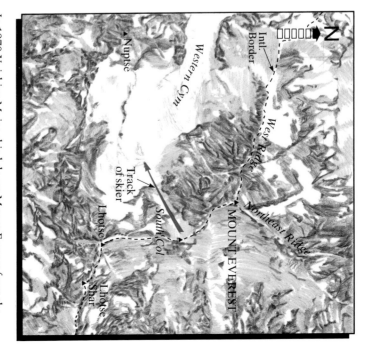

In 1970 Yuichiro Miura skied down Mount Everest from the South Col to the Western Cwm.

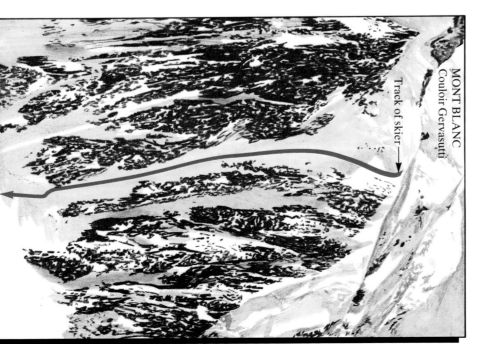

MONT BLANC
Couloir Gervasutti

Track of skier

The couloir Gervasutti on Mont Blanc du Tacul, another Saudan first.

R Guy

Sylvain Saudan, born September 1936, set the challenge for others to follow. Apart from skiing from the summit of the 26,496ft (8,068m) Hidden Peak in the Himalayas, one of his most famous 'firsts' was his 9,000ft (2,700m) descent of the Walker spur in the Grand Jorasses, France. He had to make no less than 3,500 turns!

Yuichiro Muira had once competed in the 'Flying Kilometre' at Cervinia, Italy, but he had not calculated on Himalayan conditions. When his parachute opened, it failed to slow him down. Later he wrote a fascinating book entitled *The Man who Skied Down Everest*.

Heini Holzer skiing down the Brenva spur on Mont Blanc, a 60-degree slope of approximately 3,300ft (1,000m). A fall here would probably be fatal.

TREEING

Although during previous centuries thousands of Central Europeans must have no doubt visited Scandinavia, the sport of skiing in Central Europe started, surprisingly, not in the high Alps but in the much lower Black Forest region of what is now called Western Germany. Why no Swiss or Austrian had taken back skis and used them in his native mountains long before then, remains an unsolved mystery.

The grandeur of most high mountains is often enhanced by the fringe of trees which grace their slopes

below the summer snowline. If the sport of skiing started in the trees, then perhaps it is appropriate that most good downhill pistes should finish among the trees, which they invariably do. But the number of skiing enthusiasts who go 'treeing' in the powder snow, lying deep in the shade of these frosted giants, is still remarkably few.

The grandeur of the high mountains is often enhanced by a fringe of trees.

CURLING

One way to spend a relaxing afternoon. The object is not to hit the wood – much the same as treeing!

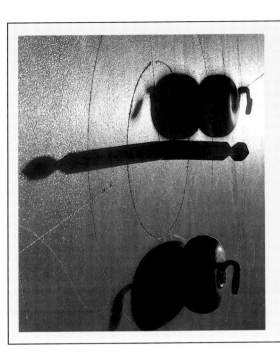

This thermal image of the central Alps in summer, taken by satellite, shows their extensive woodlands (dark areas), particularly on north-facing slopes.

Treeing of another kind. Christmas in Poland, late 1930s.

Treeing on the Zugspitze, near Garmisch-Partenkirchen, West Germany. Not the safest way, but the better way, to ski the lower slopes of the mountain.

THE LAST RUN DOWN

*L'amore di qualunque cosa e figiulo d'essa cognitione.
L'amore e tanto piu fervente quanto la cognitione e piu
certa.*

Love is the daughter of knowledge.
The profounder the knowledge the greater the love.

Leonardo da Vinci

Our love of skiing is not only enduring, but it grows each time we venture to the mountains. The sport started when there were no ski-lifts, no piste makers, no safety bindings, few guides and nowhere on the mountain to buy a drink. Yet it was not so surprising that the early pioneers returned again and again. With each year that passes there are swifter ski-lifts, safer pistes, improved bindings, more guides and more watering holes than ever before, and the opportunities for skiing, on a greater area of mountain and over a longer season, become better and better. But that is not why our love of skiing grows, certainly not in concert with the increasing herds of skiers. We know too much about lift queues and orange peel, piste bashers and rutted powder snow; our love of skiing runs much deeper than that. Perhaps not many skiers ask themselves why they return to the slopes year after year – in some cases, several times each season. But those who do usually have one overriding reason – to improve their skiing.

The greater a skier's proficiency, the more enjoyable skiing will be. There is more time to savour the crisp-clean air, to understand the intricacies of snow craft and the vagaries of high-altitude weather, more time to acknowledge the permanency of the magnificent scenery and to make friends with the mountain folk, some of the nicest people on earth. And when the holiday is over and it is time to return to the office desk or to the mud on the farm, there is always one run left to remember until the next time – the last run down.

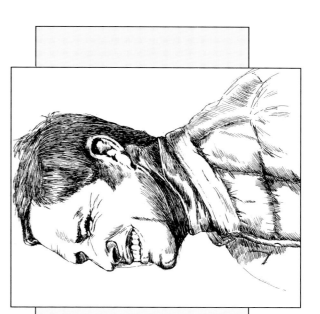

Opposite: The last run down.

Buddy Werner, one of the best-loved American ski champions, who was tragically killed with the famous Barbi Henneberger in April 1964 by an avalanche on a gentle slope at St Moritz, Switzerland, which fell from both sides of a small gully. However experienced, no skier is safe from avalanches. Knowledge of snowcraft is the greatest antidote, a bleeper and a trusty spade may give some relief, but there is no known cure. Every run off piste may be the last run down.

DRY SNOW AVALANCHES

The most devastating of all types of avalanche, the dry or powder snow avalanche generates a destructive blast of air before it, similar to a high explosive bomb. Wind speeds have been recorded of 190 mph (305 kph) and because in the swirling snow the individual flakes loose their feathers, the powder drops as a solid mass, making it difficult to dig out victims, who have not already been suffocated by ice particles, alive.

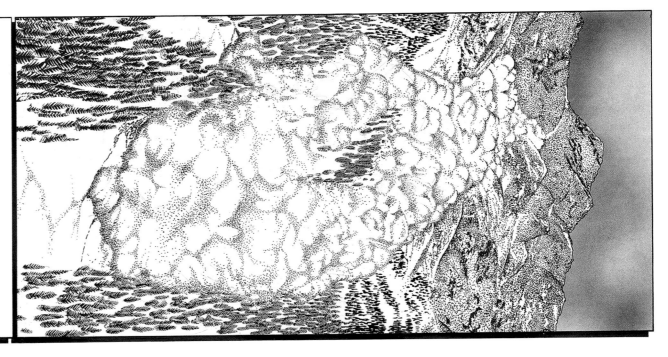

WET SNOW AVALANCHES

As the snow becomes saturated in warmer weather it often slides away from a single point of origin to ball up and roll down the mountain gathering rocks as it gains momentum. Often a skier can move faster than this type of avalanche, but should he get caught he may either get hit by debris or worse still get buried under snow with the consistency of wet concrete. A large avalanche may consist of a million tonnes of snow.

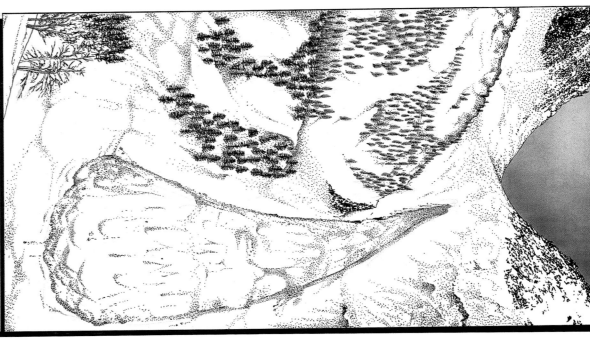

SLAB AVALANCHES

Rather than start at a single point slab avalanches break away, usually with a loud report, from large areas at once. The snow, which has probably been lying in layers, then falls as a slab, breaking into smaller pieces as it accelerates. Dry slab avalanches are often caused by wind-pack, and wet slab avalanches by water spreading over a lower layer of ice. They are difficult to avoid as they may be several hundred metres across.

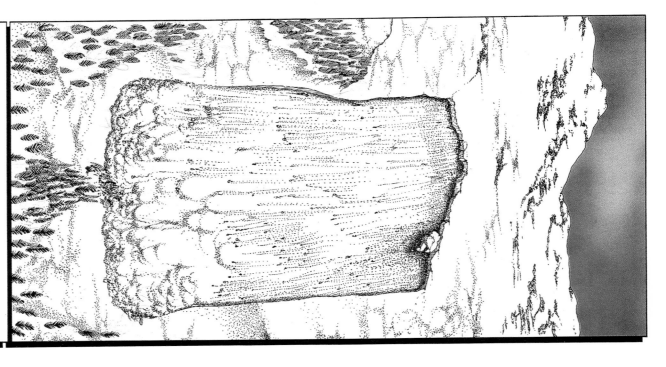

AVALANCHES

Then, from high up above him, he heard that most dreaded of all sounds in the High Alps, that rending booming crack! The Last Trump! Avalanche!

The ground shook violently under Bond's skis and the swelling rumble came down to him like the noise of express trains roaring through a hundred tunnels. God Almighty, now he really had had it! What was the rule? Point the skis straight downhill! Try and race it! Bond pointed his skis down towards the tree line, got down in his ugly crouch and shot, his skis screaming, into white space.

From On Her Majesty's Secret Service by Ian Fleming

What is the rule? For James Bond and his screaming skis the solution was probably correct, but avalanches behave differently. Much has been written about their cruel nature and how to avoid them, little about what to do when you meet one face to face.

First: don't panic. Second: try to identify its nature. A loud report normally means a slab avalanche which you may well be able to ski away from. Any other type of avalanche and you must try and ski across its path, if possible to higher ground. Third: if you have the misfortune to be engulfed, throw away your ski sticks and release your skis before they can twist you into knots. Swim like hell, then, if your head is clear of the snow, shout; if it is not, shut your mouth and fight to make a breathing space. Fourth: keep still – it uses up less oxygen – and pray.

All is not lost – but it is best to carry a spade!

A dry snow avalanche may travel faster than a skier can fall through the air.

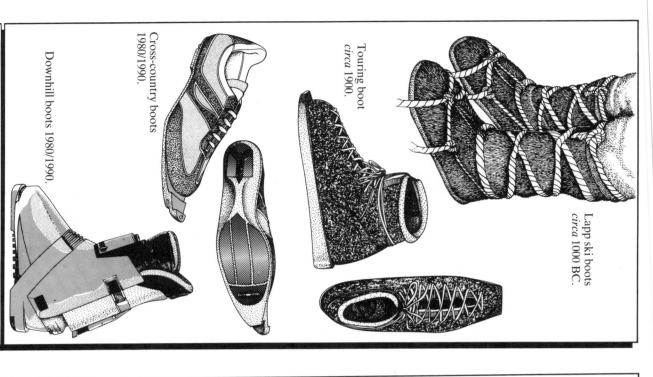

Lapp ski boots *circa* 1000 BC.

Touring boot *circa* 1900.

Cross-country boots 1980/1990.

Downhill boots 1980/1990.

To order a new lace-up leather ski boot of yesteryear would now be prohibitively expensive. Instead the modern skier must accept being clamped into two plastic vices which neither breath nor shape themselves, except through inner liners, into the 'character' of his clammy feet. Many a plastic boot has been given major surgery, which is often terminal, as a result. Cross-Country boots have always been more comfortable and later types may also be used for picking up coins dropped by passing skiers. Cosiest were the old Lapp ski boots made of soft sealskin. They may well return (see page 90).

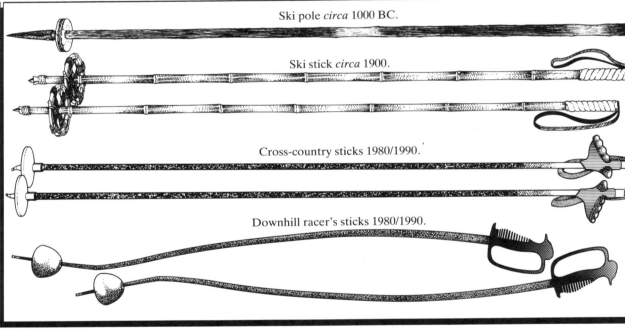

Ski pole *circa* 1000 BC.

Ski stick *circa* 1900.

Cross-country sticks 1980/1990.

Downhill racer's sticks 1980/1990.

The first ski pole was dual purpose; for skiing with and for spearing game. A bone disc stopped the pole from breaking through the snow and a sheath made of Elk hide prevented the wooden point being blunted. Subsequent pairs of sticks have not been so special. Bamboo sticks, which were all the rage until after the second World War, often split, and some new carbon fibre langlauf sticks have been under close scrutiny because of their plastic hand grips, which are said to give unfair advantage. The Downhill sticks, manufactured to curve round the body, may be bent further over the knee by overweight racers.

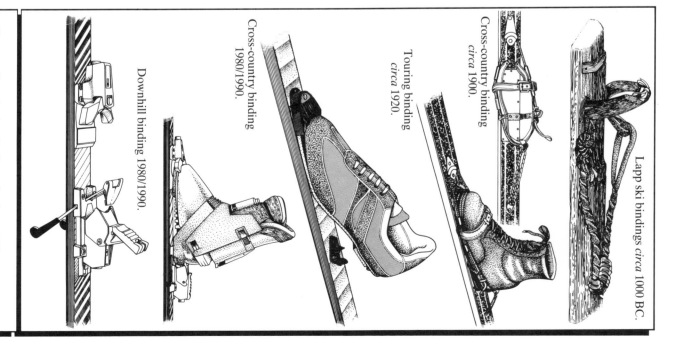

Lapp ski bindings *circa* 1000 BC.

Cross-country binding *circa* 1900.

Touring binding *circa* 1920.

Cross-country binding 1980/1990.

Downhill binding 1980/1990.

The complicated safety bindings of today, which are easy to snap on and off a modern ski boot and have a lever to stop the ski running away when released, have several disadvantages over the old type touring binding. They are expensive, it is difficult to walk in them, impossible to tour in them, and they are putting the accident clinics out of business. Modern langlauf bindings are inexpensive and cleverly designed in some cases to allow the toe of the boot to clip in underneath. But the old Lapp bindings illustrated, made of wild boar's tusks and thongs of wolf skin, take the prize for ingenuity.

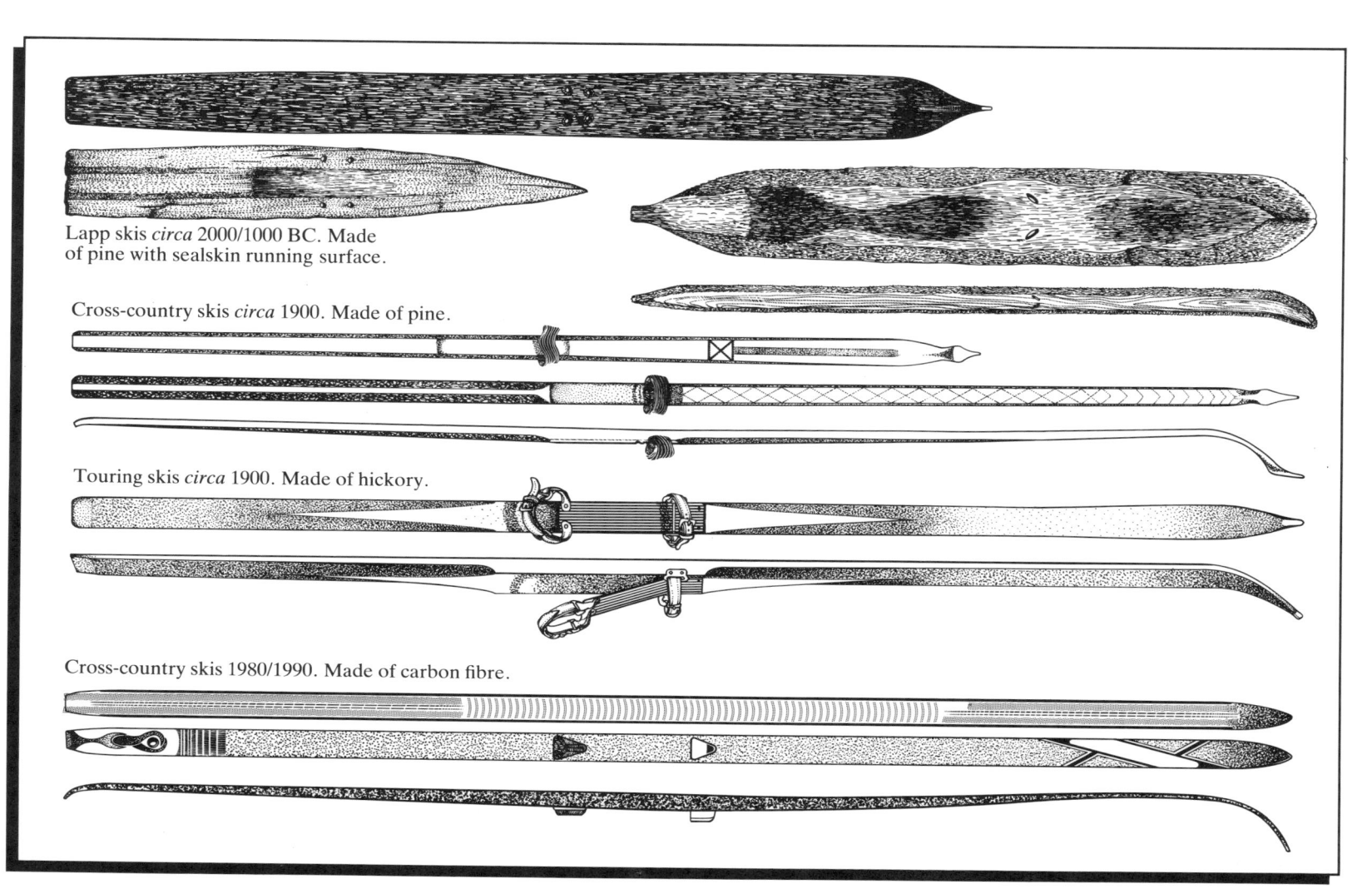

Lapp skis *circa* 2000/1000 BC. Made
of pine with sealskin running surface.

Cross-country skis *circa* 1900. Made of pine.

Touring skis *circa* 1900. Made of hickory.

Cross-country skis 1980/1990. Made of carbon fibre.

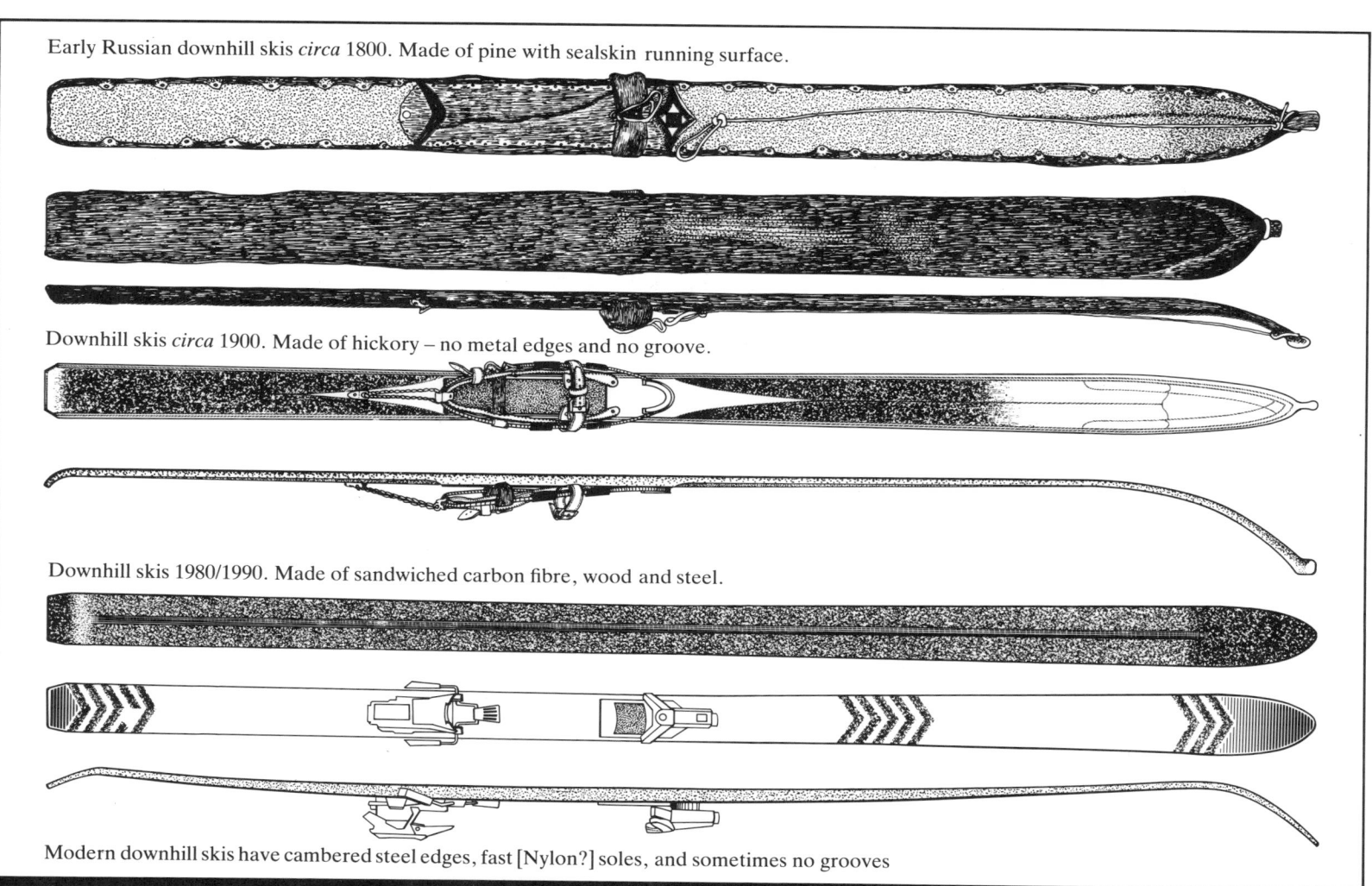

Early Russian downhill skis *circa* 1800. Made of pine with sealskin running surface.

Downhill skis *circa* 1900. Made of hickory – no metal edges and no groove.

Downhill skis 1980/1990. Made of sandwiched carbon fibre, wood and steel.

Modern downhill skis have cambered steel edges, fast [Nylon?] soles, and sometimes no grooves

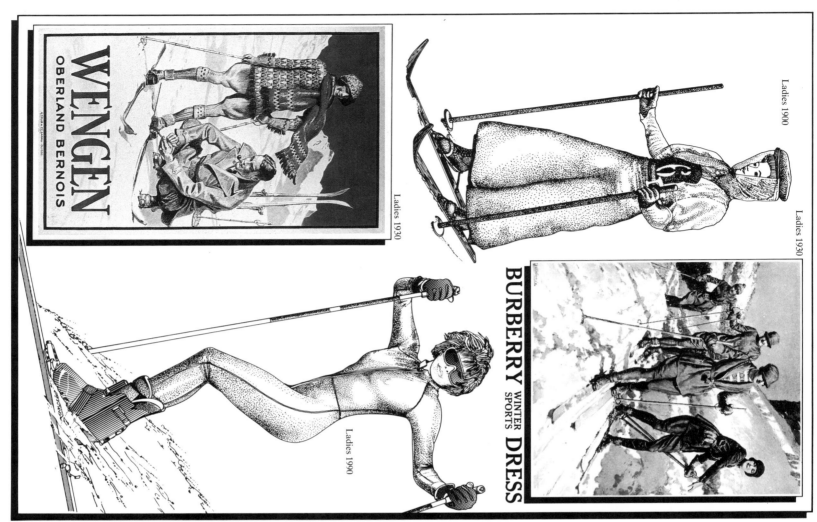

Ladies 1900

Ladies 1930

Ladies 1930

Ladies 1990

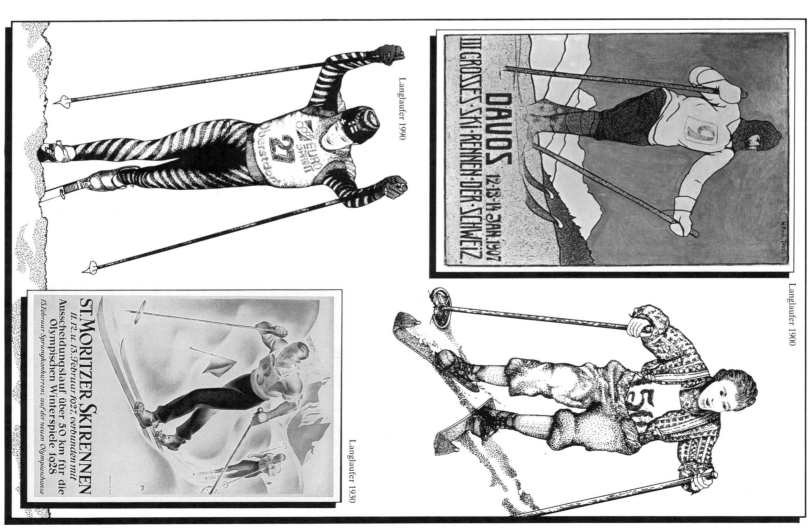

Langlaufer 1990

Langlaufer 1900

Langlaufer 1900

Langlaufer 1930

Downhiller 1930

Downhiller 1990

Downhiller 1950

MÜRREN

DIE RENNTAGE DER KANONEN

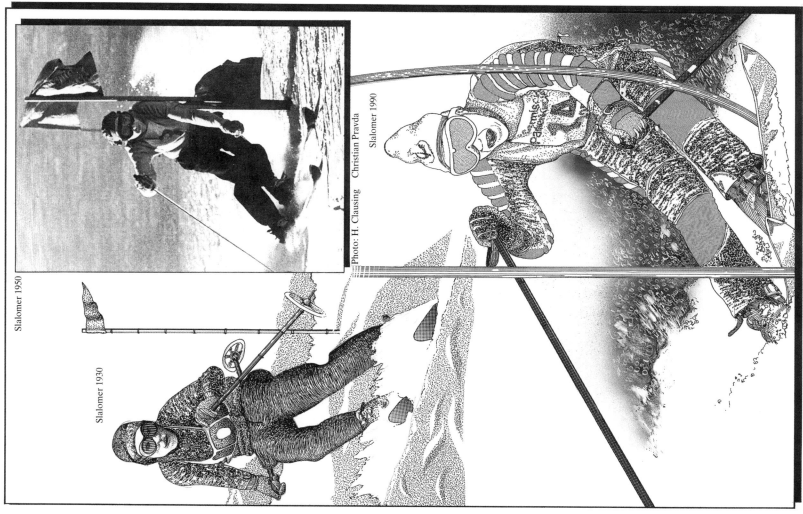

Slalomer 1950

Slalomer 1930

Slalomer 1990

Photo: H. Clausing   Christian Pravda

A French railway poster.

An old type rack-and-pinion railway.

MOUNTAIN TRANSPORT

The first railway in Switzerland was not opened, surprisingly, until June 1844, and the country was not blessed with a complete 1,000 mile rail system much before the end of the nineteenth century. Thus skiing and ski transport in Switzerland grew up hand in hand and, as in other alpine countries, many railway coaches were built with skiers very much in mind. Today on the track from the end of the road at Tasch to Zermatt, for example, a special drive-on train is provided for both trolleys and skis.

Some of the first primitive drag-lifts were constructed in the United States in the early 1930s and these were followed by the first chairlift at Sun Valley in 1936. Cableways had long been used for carrying minerals, but not until the middle of this century was the principle applied to passenger transport in America. At about this time the Sunrise Peak Aerial Railway – the 'World's Grandest Scenic Route' – was born, otherwise advertised as 'To the clouds in a Bucket'. One attempt had been made to construct a *Luftseilbahn* in Switzerland in 1908, the Wetterhorn Aerial Railway, but the first successful cableway was not completed until 1927 at Engelberg, few others being installed by ski resorts before 1950. The development of the chairlift, or *Sesselbahn*, in the Alps also started at Engelberg, but as late as 1944. The *Gondelbahn*, or two- to four-seater suspended cabin, was first introduced at Crans near Montana, Switzerland, in 1951. But although all three types of aerial ski-lift had many advantages, certainly in construction cost, over the older rack-and-pinion type of transport such as that shown on a postcard here, they had one serious disadvantage – lack of passenger carrying capacity.

In 1985 a new type of ski transport was unveiled at Saas Fee in Switzerland. Not unlike the original express funicular railway built at Kaprun, Austria, in 1973, which is pulled up the face of the mountain by a cable rather than a cog, most of these second-generation funiculars are designed to travel sub-glacial, carrying up to 300 passengers at more than 30mph (48kph). Their capacity, in excess of 3,000 skiers per hour, competes favourably with the latest *Luftseilbahns* and there are no environmental problems or restrictions on operating in high winds. In France, many ski resort operators are currently tunnelling like badgers, but some skiers may find the new 'metros' even more claustrophobic than the 'swinging sardine cans' from which they can at least look out of the windows.

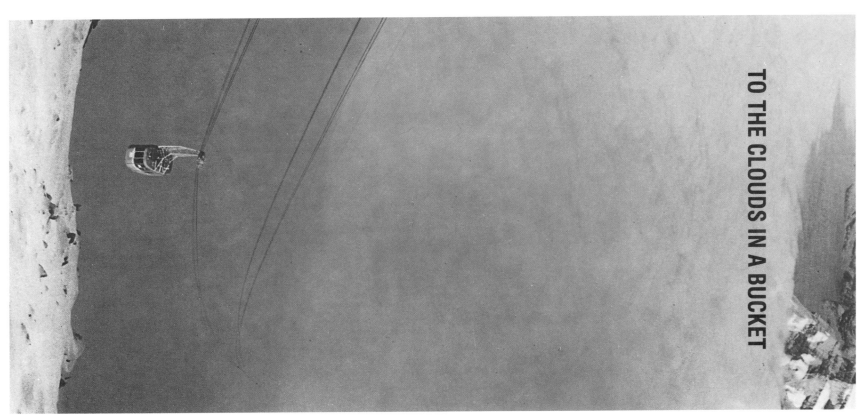

TO THE CLOUDS IN A BUCKET

An early method of getting up the mountain. America, 1930s.

Door-to-door service.

GRAND PRIX HORSE RACE
By AIR to ST. MORITZ
F.I.S. SKI RACES

Ski school 1937.
Note those already setting off up the mountain.

Most parents would never buy ski-lift tickets until their family had spent at least two days, each season, sweating up the mountainside, not because they had started skiing themselves when there were no lifts, but, so they said, to strengthen the right muscles. Today such a proliferation of ski-lifts criss-cross the mountains that few would consider such 'niceties'. Wise parents ensure that tuning up is done at home followed on the slopes – as is normal in America – by a period of solid ski instruction.

Fortunately the majority of ski instructors no longer teach their national style like 'little Hitlers'. Even the Austrians, whose technique is still the most talked about, admit that there is no longer a great difference between their own methods of instruction and those of other countries. Better they say, to teach beginners just to enjoy themselves, which taken literally gets them into all kinds of trouble. One of the best pranks at ski-school was secretly to tie all woolly ski hats to the hanging straps in the cablecar; when the doors were opened at the top and the unfortunate passengers rushed for the door, their hats were left gently swinging inside!

87

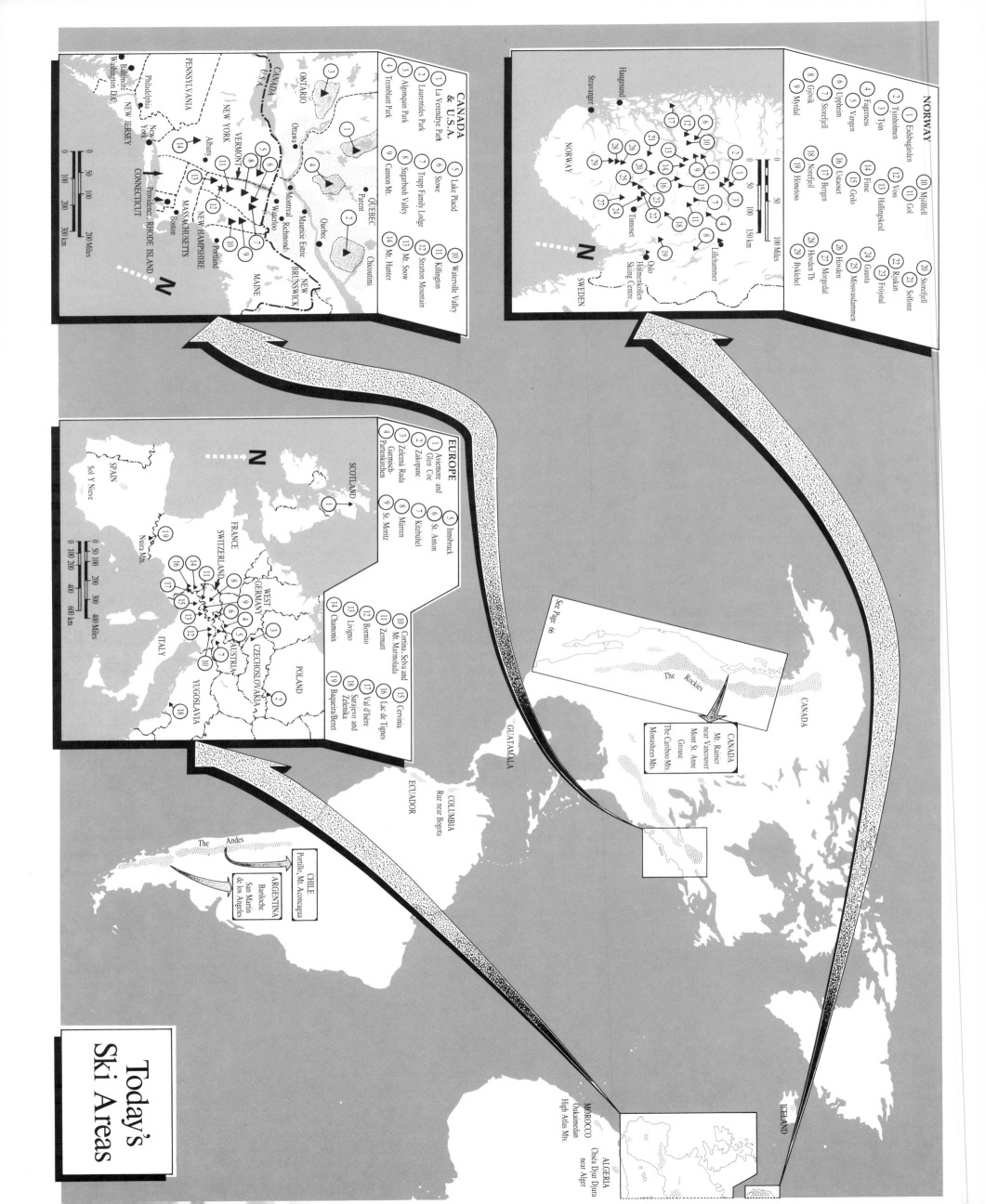

Today's Ski Areas

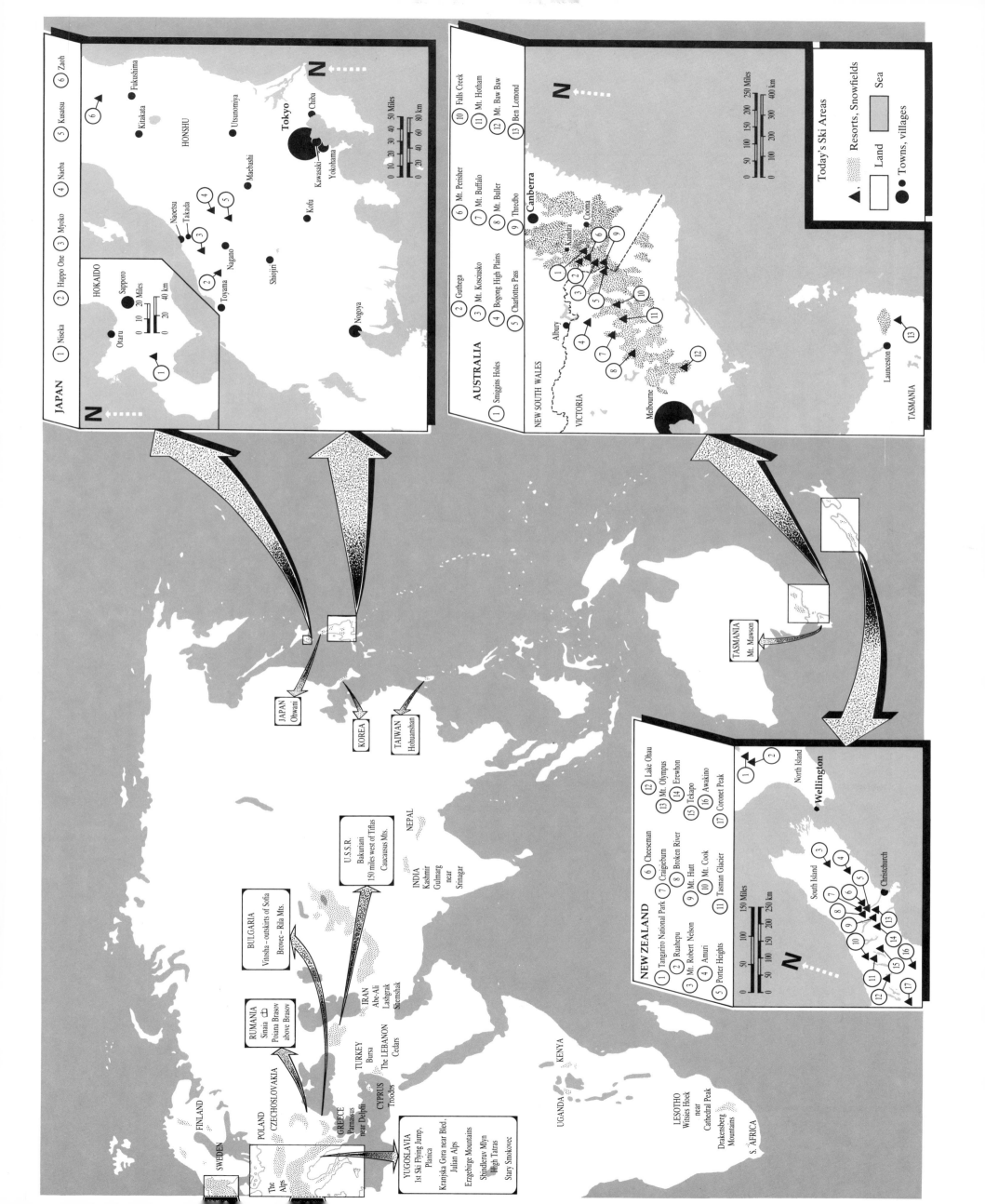

Today's Ski Areas

	Resorts, Snowfields
	Land
	Sea
	Towns, villages

JAPAN

N

HOKKAIDO

① Niseko
② Happo One
③ Myoko
④ Nacha
⑤ Kusatsu
⑥ Zaoh

Otaru
Sapporo

0 10 20 Miles
0 20 40 km

① Niseka

HONSHU

Fukushima
Kitakata
Utsunomiya
Naoetsu
Takada
④
⑤
③
② Toyama
Nagano
Maebashi
Shiojin
Kofu
Nagoya
Chiba
Kawasaki
Yokohama
Tokyo

0 10 20 30 40 Miles
0 20 40 60 80 Km

AUSTRALIA

N

① Smiggins Holes
② Guthega
③ Mt. Kosciusko
④ Bogong High Plains
⑤ Charlottes Pass
⑥ Mt. Perisher
⑦ Mt. Buffalo
⑧ Mt. Buller
⑨ Thredbo
⑩ Falls Creek
⑪ Mt. Hotham
⑫ Mt. Baw Baw
⑬ Ben Lomond

NEW SOUTH WALES

Canberra
Kiandra
Cooma
⑥
⑨
Albury
①
②
③
④
⑤
⑩
⑦
⑧
⑪
⑫

VICTORIA

Melbourne

TASMANIA

Launceston
⑬

0 50 100 150 200 250 Miles
0 100 200 300 400 km

JAPAN
Ohwani

KOREA

TAIWAN
Hohuanshan

U.S.S.R.
Bakuriani
150 miles west of Tiflis
Caucasus Mts.

NEPAL

INDIA
Kashmir
Gulmarg
near
Srinagar

BULGARIA
Vitosha – outskirts of Sofia
Brovec – Rila Mts.

RUMANIA
Sinaia ⊕
Poiana Brasov
above Brasov

IRAN
Abe-Ali
Lashgrak
Shemshak

TURKEY
Bursa

The LEBANON
Cedars

CYPRUS
Troodos

GREECE
Parnassus
near Delphi

YUGOSLAVIA
1st Ski Flying Jump,
Planica
Kranjska Gora near Bled.
Julian Alps
Erzebirge Mountains
Shindlerw Mlyn
High Tatras
Stary Smokovec

FINLAND
SWEDEN
POLAND
CZECHOSLOVAKIA

The Alps

UGANDA
KENYA

LESOTHO
Witsies Hoek
near
Cathedral Peak

S. AFRICA
Drakensberg
Mountains

TASMANIA
Mt. Mawson

NEW ZEALAND

N

North Island

Wellington

① Tangariro National Park
② Ruahepu
③ Mt. Robert Nelson
④ Amuri
⑤ Porter Heights
⑥ Cheeseman
⑦ Craigieburn
⑧ Broken River
⑨ Mt. Hutt
⑩ Mt. Cook
⑪ Tasman Glacier
⑫ Lake Ohau
⑬ Mt. Olympus
⑭ Erewhon
⑮ Tekapo
⑯ Awakino
⑰ Coronet Peak

South Island

Christchurch

①
②
③
④
⑤
⑥
⑦
⑧
⑨
⑩
⑪
⑫
⑬
⑭
⑮
⑯
⑰

0 50 100 150 Miles
0 50 100 150 200 250 km

THE FUTURE

It will not be long before there are some 50 million people skiing the world's snowfields. Longer holidays and improved mountain transport systems are bound to encourage a growing number of young people to put on skis, but nothing will excite them more than the rapidly increasing availability of slopes spread with man-made snow. In particular the Australian, recently patented, Permasnow, which although 99 per cent water is sprayed on as frozen foam has a great future for indoor ski slopes such as the author's Skidrome. Many such centres are already being planned in Japan and it will not be long before they are to be seen everywhere. As ski racing increasingly becomes sponsored by companies other than ski manufacturers, there is also likely to be a change to much lighter and more practical equipment which, hopefully, will do away with the clumsy ski boots we suffer in today.

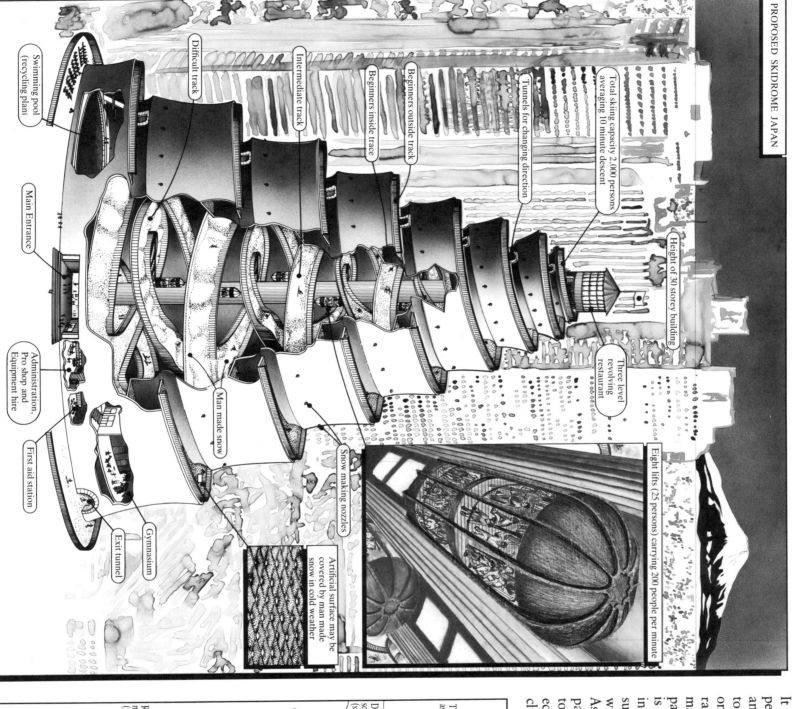

PROPOSED SKIDROME JAPAN

Difficult track

Swimming pool (recycling plant)

Intermediate track

Beginners inside trace

Beginners outside track

Tunnels for changing direction

Total skiing capacity 2,000 persons averaging 10 minute descent

Height of 30 storey building

Three level revolving restaurant

Man made snow

Eight lifts (25 persons) carrying 200 people per minute

Main Entrance

Administration, Pro shop and Equipment hire

First aid station

Gymnasium

Exit tunnel

Snow making nozzles

Artificial surface may be covered by man made snow in cold weather

Skidrome. Heat from the cooling system is used to warm the swimming pool.

Next generation equipment.

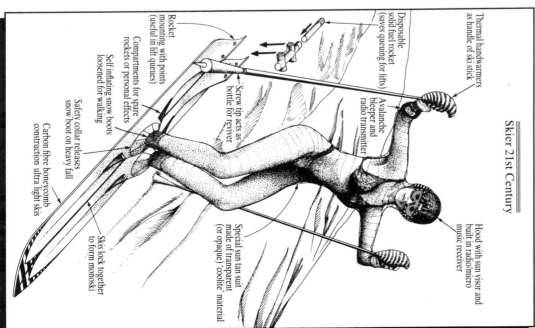

Skier 21st Century

Thermal handwarmers as handle of ski stick

Rocket mounting with points (useful in lift queues)

Disposable solid fuel rocket (saves queuing for lifts)

Screw tip acts as bottle for reviver

Avalanche bleeper and radio transmitter

Compartments for spare rockets or personal effects

Self inflating snow boots loosened for walking

Safety collar releases snow boot on heavy fall

Carbon fibre honeycomb construction ultra light skis

Skis lock together to form monoski

Special sun tan suit made of transparent (or opaque) 'coolie' material

Hood with sun visor and built in radio/micro music receiver

Skiing in the twenty-first century.

91

CHRONOLOGY OF SKIING

2500BC Estimated date of 'Hoting ski' discovered in a Swedish peat bog

2500BC Skis found in the Altai Mountains in Khasakstan, Russia

2000BC Estimated date of rock impression of skier found at Roedoey, Norway

555 Byzantine historian Procopius mentions *skridfinnen* (gliding) Finns

800 Earliest written account of skis by Chinese in history of T'ang Dynasty

1070 Bishop Adam of Bremen sights northern hunters 'borne on bent boards'

1206 Two Norwegian *Birkebeiner* ski with King Sverre's infant son to safety

1274 The hunting of deer on skis is forbidden in Norway

1520 Gustav Vasa skis to Mora, Sweden, to lead his troops against the Danes

1664 Francesco Negri of Ravenna, first Central European to ski in Scandinavia

1716 First company of élite ski troops formed in Norway

1722 Scandinavians introduce skis to Greenland

1733 A military ski-manual produced for the first time

1759 Skis first seen in Canada, at an ice carnival

1808 Norway goes to war with Sweden with over 2,000 ski troops

1825 The *Restoration* sails from Stavanger to the New World carrying skis

1840 Sondre Norheim, of Telemark, is the first to make a recognised ski jump

1843 Competition with cross-country, jumping and downhill at Tromsö, Norway

1849 Norwegian sailors looking for gold, set out with skis from San Francisco

1856 'Snowshoe Thompson' starts delivering mail on skis in California

1857 A Norwegian labourer brings skiing to Ontario, Canada

1859 Skis first seen in Switzerland at Sils Maria in the Engadine

1861 Very first ski club in the world founded in Kiandra, Australia

1862 Norwegian miners bring skis to the Otago goldfields in New Zealand

1864 First winter sportsmen invited to the Alps by J. Badrutt of St Moritz

1867 The first United States ski club formed at La Porte, California

1877 The Norwegian Christiania Ski club hold the first ever ski meeting. Sondre Norheim demonstrates the telemark and christiania turns

1879 First recorded Swedish ski-jumping competition

1884 Nordenskiold Ski Race. First major cross-country event in the world

1887 Skiing first introduced to Czechoslovakia

1888 Fridtjof Nansen traverses Greenland on skis

1890 Norwegian settlers deliver mail from Argentina over the Andes to Chile

1891 Mathias Zdarsky starts skiing in the Black forest region of Germany

1892 Skiing competitions first held at Holmenkollen, near Oslo, Norway

1895 The first German ski club formed in the Black Forest, Germany

1896 Mathias Zdarsky opens his 'Lilienfeld School', the first ever ski school

1897 Mathias Zdarsky publishes his *Technique of Skiing*. Wilhelm Paulcke and party traverse the Bernese Oberland on skis

1898 Arnold Lunn takes friends to Chamonix and starts the ski-holiday trade

1899 Norwegian missionaries take their skis to China

1901 Davos ski club formed in Switzerland. First Italian ski club formed at Turin

1902 Skiing introduced to Japan by Norwegian Consul, Petter Ottesen

1903 Ski Club of Great Britain formed in London. First recorded ski race ever held in the Alps at Davos, Switzerland

1904 First meeting of the Montreal Ski Club. First Spanish ski club formed at Guadarrama

1905 First slalom race, held by Zdarsky on the Muckenkogel, Austria

1906 First skikjöring race held at St Moritz, Switzerland

1908 Norwegian Ski Federation founded

1911 The Roberts of Kandahar. First downhill race held at Montana in Switzerland

1913 Ruapehu Ski Club founded in New Zealand

1921 British Championships at Scheidegg, Switzerland. First downhill race set

1922 First 'modern slalom', organised by Arnold Lunn at Mürren, Switzerland

1922 The Vasa cross-country race inaugurated in Sweden

1924 Fédération Internationale de Ski (FIS) founded at Chamonix, France. First Winter World Championships for Nordic skiing. First Winter Olympic Games held at Chamonix, France. The Kandahar Ski Club founded at Mürren, Switzerland

1925 First World Championships in cross-country skiing and jumping. National Ski Association of Japan (SAJ) founded. Downhill Only Club, DHO, founded at Wengen, Switzerland

1927 Hannes Schneider, ski school instructor at St Anton, Austria, meets Arnold Lunn

1928 Arnold Lunn organises the first Arlberg–Kandahar meeting. II Winter Olympic Games held at St Moritz, Switzerland

1930 Ski Club of Chile founded

1931 First FIS Alpine Championships held at Mürren, Switzerland. The Parsenn funicular railway built for skiers at Davos, Switzerland

1932 III Winter Olympic Games held at Lake Placid, USA. The first drag-lift in the USA installed at Woodstock, Vermont

LIST OF PLATES

Enquiries about paintings still on exhibition, or about reproductions, may be made to: Robert Guy, Ashcombe Tower, Dawlish, Devon, England.

ACKNOWLEDGEMENTS

The Story of Skiing could not have been written, and the dramatic scenes painted, without the tremendous help given by Elizabeth Hussey and Camilla Buxton of the Ski Club of Great Britain, which has the most complete library of books and periodicals about the sport in the world. Paul Maxlow-Tomlinson, until recently the club's chairman, gave up his valuable time to read through the proofs, for which I am equally indebted.

I would never have completed the script without the wealth of information so kindly given by the ever helpful Peter Kasper, Director of the Kurverein in St Moritz, and his son Gian Franco Kasper, Secretary General of the Fédération Internationale de Ski, whom I quizzed at the FIS headquarters in Berne, Switzerland. My special thanks go to Peter Lunn, the distinguished skier and son of Sir Arnold, who encouraged me greatly in my research, and to Ted Varley, another generous contributor from Mürren.

In the United States I was fortunate to be entertained at Stratton Mountain, Vermont, by my friend and President of its parent company Moore & Munger, David Rosow. Eno Henrich and his team there could not have been more informative about skiing on the East Coast. I am also most grateful to the management at Aspen and Vail, Colorado, for their help in compiling the pages about skiing in the Rockies.

I received invaluable advice from Dr Med Fred Auer, St Moritz, Switzerland; Eva Carlsson of the Svenska Skidförbundet; Ekkehart Ulmrich of the Deutscher Skiverband; Jan Vedral of the Československý Svaz Lyžařů; Professor Hoppichler of the Bundessportheim and Heinrich Wagner of the Fremdenverkehrsverband, St Anton, Austria; Bruce Carnall of the Canadian Ski Association and Bill Tindale of the Canadian Ski Museum; Peter Southwell-Keely of the Kosciusko Alpine Club, Australia; Philip Rogers of the Aorangi Ski Club; Peter Dady of the Ruapehu Mountain Club and Frank Drewitt of the New Zealand Ski Association, not forgetting Ted Ohashi of the Ski Association of Japan.

Finally I would like to thank all those who assisted in the book's production, particularly the young artist Robert Guy, who undoubtedly has a great future ahead of him, Ethan Danielson, who produced the superb line drawings, and my untiring secretary Jackie, who has added some splendid portraits. Last, but not least, I thank my long-suffering wife Annette for her patience in the mountains.

Nous créons pour le ciel, les parfums, les oiseaux,
nous créons pour les montagnes et la tempête,
nous créons pour nous perdre aux vents et aux soleils,
nous créons pour frôler les immenses sommeils,
jusqu'à ce que lassés de ces dons inutiles
et magnifiques, nous quittons nos skis faciles.
Mais nous les reprendons ces divins créatures
pour de clairs tournoiements aux mondes séducteurs,
jusqu'à laisser un jour sur la neige éternelle,
pour une fois encore à notre âme fidèle,
la trace où le désir en lui se finira,
la trace où notre vie en elle se perdra!...

From *les skieurs*, Jean Bordeaux, 1930

96